FAWZI KARIM

Plague Lands and other poems

Versions by Anthony Howell
after translations by Abbas Kadhim

With an introduction by Elena Lappin
and an afterword by Marius Kociejowski

CARCANET

First published in Great Britain in 2011 by
Carcanet Press Limited
Alliance House
Cross Street
Manchester M2 7AQ

A CIP catalogue record for this book is available from the British Library

ISBN 978 1 84777 063 9

The publisher acknowledges financial assistance from Arts Council England

Supported by
ARTS COUNCIL
ENGLAND

Typeset by XL Publishing Services, Tiverton
Printed and bound in England by SRP Ltd, Exeter

Contents

Introduction

Like all powerful totalitarian regimes, Saddam Hussein's long reign produced a defiant dissident culture in exile. The fate of numerous Iraqi intellectuals who escaped Ba'thist censorship and continued to write in diaspora is not as well known as the activities of various Iraqi opposition groups, though it ought to be.

One deeply influential and much-loved poet of the exiled generation is Fawzi Karim, an Iraqi Shi'ite who was born in Baghdad in 1945 and has been living in London since 1978. Karim's sense of internal exile began long before he left Iraq, when he found himself outside all the ideological movements sweeping the intellectual life of his country. Karim was neither Communist nor Ba'thist nor religious nor anarchist. Nor was his poetry influenced by the Western avant-garde or by surrealism, as was the work of many of his peers. This non-political and deeply individualistic stance was a dangerous one in Saddam's Iraq, and an unusual one even among Iraqi artists in exile.

By the time Karim left Baghdad, he had become known for his independent thinking and his dislike of Ba'thist ideology, expressed during hours spent in cafés and bars with fellow poets and writers. He was no longer allowed to publish even innocuous pieces of journalism, such as book reviews, under his own name. His subversive ideas were a variation on one theme: you can either be a poet or a Ba'thist, but you can't be both. Although he was not the only Iraqi poet with a hatred of ideology, he became the most persistent defender of a poet's need for political freedom, devoting a book of essays to the subject (which has not been published in English).

In 1993, Kanan Makiya, a leading Iraqi dissident intellectual, quoted the following poem by Fawzi Karim in his seminal book on Saddam's rule, *Cruelty and Silence*, as an example of a defiantly personal voice in an era of dehumanisation:

> Each sail not counted as yours, oh policeman of the border,
> Sailing not in useless search for The Meaning
> But fleeing from all those black meanings,
> Know that it is mine.

As Makiya saw it, without individualistic, non-ideological writing such as Karim's, 'a morbid hatred of the West and Israel is going to remain the focus of increasingly degraded notions of "Arabness" or "Islamic identity"'.

This poem was written in 1979, Karim's first year in London (where he ultimately established himself as a columnist for *al-Mutamar*, the London-based Iraqi opposition newspaper, and for the international Arab daily *al-Sharq al-Awsat*). He had left behind a country in which his very poor neighbourhood and family home had been razed by the Ba'thists to make room for luxurious gardens for Saddam's palaces. In Iraq, his days as a free writer were numbered; most of his friends who had refused to collaborate with the regime and had not emigrated would soon be dead, as a result either of torture or illness. (Karim himself suffered a serious heart attack a few months after arriving in England, when he was in his thirties.)

Karim's poetry is particularly interesting for its unusual combination of free form and classical language. In the 1940s, free verse was introduced into Iraqi poetry, under the influence of T.S. Eliot and Ezra Pound. After more than 2,000 years of following a strict symmetrical metre, Iraqi poets found an entirely new style of writing, which then spread from Iraq throughout the rest of the Arab world. Though Karim writes in free verse, his use of Arabic is uncompromisingly rooted in the linguistic complexity and tradition of the Quran (although his poetry is entirely devoid of religious content). Perhaps unsurprisingly, the burdens of exile and of memory are two of his recurring themes; Karim writes about human tragedy in all its 'demasked nakedness' and vulnerability. But these are not abstract ideas: he writes about them, and the death and loss of friends, family, and home, in the context of his life. He also believes in a profound link between poetry and music and sings his poems as he writes them.

For the new generation, Fawzi Karim represents the conscience of the deeply wounded Iraqi culture: a reminder that it was once possible to write without fear, and now will be again. A few years ago, a younger poet who had violently disagreed with Karim about the need to choose between poetry and ideology organised a well-attended public reading in Baghdad, at which he read a poem he dedicated, or rather addressed, to Karim: a personal confession about the mistake he'd made in believing that ideological commitment was compatible with the freedom of being a poet. Although some younger readers find Karim's rich verse difficult to decipher, his moral fearlessness in a time of spiritual and political repression has won him wide readership in Iraq, and his return is eagerly anticipated. (He now plans on dividing his time between Baghdad and London.)

All political movements, including democratic ones, are couched in intellectual thought, yet the complex role of intellectuals in the birth of totalitarian regimes is a rarely explored theme in modern cultural history, from Stalinist Russia to Nazi Germany. The irony tends to be deep and painful; the regimes usually turn on those whose words and ideas had served as their initial sources of inspiration. (The most poignant example of such a writer is the Czech novelist Milan Kundera, whose writing career began in the 1950s with ideological (Marxist) poetry denouncing the émigré as a traitor, but soon blossomed – at home and in exile – into a major literary oeuvre exploring the themes of memory, exile, and the effect of totalitarianism on the human soul.) Fawzi Karim believes that, as part of the post-Saddam revival of Iraq, Iraqi intellectuals must understand and accept their own culpability. 'Saddam did not emerge out of nowhere by accident,' he told me. 'He was an evil tree planted by ourselves, *as* intellectuals, in the 1950s, when we began to define our life as a struggle between various, mostly left-wing ideologies. All of us intellectuals contributed to preparing the ground for Saddam Hussein. And we are shocked and don't feel responsible! Yet I think we *are* responsible.'

Saddam Hussein had a fear of the written word, like all dictators, and controlled it as ruthlessly as he controlled human life. But while Iraqi writers were persecuted, Saddam paid lavish monthly salaries to other Arab writers, in many countries, in exchange for celebratory prose and poetry. The lists of these writers have now become available and will be published in Iraq. The position of Iraqi intellectuals in the new political climate will be very different from their counterparts in other Arab countries. Karim says: 'We should now learn to treat political ideologies not as secular religion to be subscribed to blindly and used as weapons, but as interesting books; we should study them, and then put them back on the shelf, where they belong. For this, we will need a lot of time, and patience. But I am an Iraqi poet: my time is like water.'

Elena Lappin

Plague Lands

Part One

Channels maintained by the rain…
Houses as precarious as stacked-up disks of bread;
Their window-nets like tattered sieves;
Their doors holding their breath in case there's a call in the night;
The power cables droning with the current of suppressed desires
And the alleys twisted, just like a warrior's braids.
The Tigris will nudge us with its epics
And, with its wand, expose the deceit
     of burdened skies that weep for the days on end.
Fish leap out at their observers;
Bury their heads in their garments' folds,
And, having secreted their eggs there, give up the ghost.
Ripples drench the pores of our mutual yearning
     with the scent of myth.
Ripples caress our pillows in the night hours,
And mirrors alternate with the sun in searing our bodies.
Ripples throw up the smell of dung, palm pollen, rushes and clay,
Willows, the furnace's mouth,
The ominous cry of a crow behind a fence,
Reeds and silt and the scent of al-Khidr candles.
Sacrificed blood stains the tunnel of my boyhood:
     the one that leads to the myth.
At the entrance to an alley – out of which poured everything –
     I imagined Gilgamesh.
Go pluck a bloom from the home-grown oleander
And sell its scent to the vendor.

On the day that I was born,
While my mother remained unconscious
And my father began to prepare for the flood,
A world war ground to its halt.

At this mighty junction of deteriorating time
We were naively growing up reckless.
We would salute that oleander, hot with our uniqueness:
A family of diverse individuals – distinguished by our father's face,
While our mother's linked us like a many-blossomed tamarisk.
Who can blame my brother for discouraging
        my insatiable self-curiosity?
Who can blame my mother for nourishing
        my yen for some unreachable fantasy?

The girls next door are not to blame,
        nor are the boys with dreams laid low
        because of the revolution.
No one's to blame.
Though the eye turns black as night itself,
And the days are knots in barbed wire.

My father died, and my mother died.
And the oleander was used for firewood.
No one's to blame:
Neither the wrongdoer nor the one wronged;
Neither the thief nor his mark;
Neither the adulterers nor the ones who stone their homes.
I can't fault the sun for scorching me...

But there are the cats that would pounce from behind
        the black backdrop of fate:
The black cats that spit, that are fevered, that pounce
Under the skin of the mask of the face of the darkness;
Cats that keep pouncing, keep scratching my face,
Their claws in a scrabble for lost chords scratched from the voice.

The soul cats pounce
In silence, as if the house had vanished,
As if hundreds of towns
	and whole countries
Had vanished;
Utterly shrunk by horizons shutting them down.

No one can blame the mystic, who pokes the nipple and mutters,
	'The truth is out!'
While she exposes a pair of innocent breasts.
No one is ever to blame, for desire is a can of worms!
Or, in my case, book-worms, I guess.
I read *The Book of Beasts* by al-Jahiz
And *The Perfumed Garden*.
I read *The Trials of Destiny* quite deeply, and the *Lives*,
With *The Fruits of Literature* beside me.
I then wrote a book
On *The Classification of Souls in the Monastery of Solitude*
That dealt with those gone astray in the maze of the state.
And I wrote an *Elucidation of Certain Alexandrianisms
	in Verse Wanderings by Bewitched Waters*,
And on *The Soul's Transcendence of Sexual Repression*.
The margin is reserved for a book on the untold,
	though I haven't written this yet.
But this is why I was never awed
	by my Sufi friend in the Café Ibrahim,
Nor silenced by the dogma of my friend the revolutionary,
	fashioning a slogan from some principle.
As for debate in the bar at the Gardenia,
All I ever wanted was a drink.

Summer was heavy, heavy…
The dead more fatigued by the sun than the quick.
It takes a stiff arak to fortify the mind
    against the slow rot of a rigid daily round
And pickle one till tougher than the grass
They set ablaze with slogans and the flags that come to pass.

'Things in the bar seem to hug one another:
This table, that chair, the leftovers from the appetiser,
The water from some thawed ice a crescent at my heel,
The shadow cast, and the warmth of the hand
    still holding the emptied glass.
Do you hear a voice? The waves
Go pounding through my head. Drowning's on the cards.
Things hug one another.'

War detonates as Baghdad sets out for the markets.
I was born, I think, in a mellower year;
A year when people still paused at the smell of corpses.
Now I smell the roasting of a thigh,
And the deep voice: 'That roasting thigh is a traitor's.'
He pours on more kerosene
And the fire glows and the smell of flesh gets stronger.
My brother and I began as the chanters of slogans.
We saw the world with its trousers down and laughed.
We opened vents for the smell in our shackled bodies
And the smell disappeared within us.
That revolutionary summer had just such a smell.
And my father said, 'Whoever goes sniffing out corpses
    would want to be rid of their stench.'

My father was never wrong. But it was a mellower year
A year when people still paused. A year
That saw the barrier go down between me and that smell,
Between me and the era, between me and its dogma.

Summer shows Baghdad in its true colours:
In these, the stars of the military shine,
To emerge at dawn as a crown of thorns
Placed on the people's grey.
Their brows are the archive
Testifying to the pronouncements of the revolution.
Bitter the ordeals it engenders.

And poetry, shaven of pate, shepherds everything, high on a hill.
A rural man with a flowing gown,
How striking he looks, as the sun sets: one who enjoys his aloneness.
One with a view about everything, just as he sees fit:
'I am at one with the breeze, and this is how I am.'
But poetry departs, when under threat; heads for
The snow-capped peaks. Poetry always departs,
Its shrinking silhouette ever decried as apathy.
Now I shall partake of the forebodings of al-Rumi,
Enter the house occupied by the clairvoyant in the verse of al-Tayyib,
Lock myself into the cages of Abu Tammam,
And, orphaned, I'll tend prohibited fruit in the orchard of Abu Nuwas
While tearfully striking sparks from the *Saqt al-Zand*.
And I shall descend, with punters such as Baghdadi,
Into the dens of the poor who wear nothing but shadows,
As Ibn Nabata would reel from the dens of Shorja
Enwreathed in the heady aroma of spices and debt.

Penny-wise, they say.
But what if you seriously need
To become well-off?
It was Iraq that betrayed us,
Although we never exposed it to much
Beyond the pain of our leaving.

Now, as if covertly,
Abu al-Hasan al-Sallami
Tails this departure, and that one,
While a sugared trace of Ibn Sokara –
Finely-featured, powdered clown, *auguste* –
Perches, perches moon-like, on the fence.

Neither our crown prince nor caliph,
                    Nevertheless, you snubbed us!
Keep up the snobbery, I say,
                    For I have no pay you can stop.
Why hold a job for the losing?
                    Not that this makes me perfect.
Paragons of virtue get accused.
                    Poetry alone is a burning without smoke,
Though certain rhymes do have their undertones.
                    A few light words can wreck a reputation,
And, however delicate the musk,
                    Larded on, it can become a stench.

Then Ibn al-Hajjaj reiterates his low laugh:
'I fled from my home to a country,
Where the famine turned my pecker yellow.'

Famine turns the pecker yellow! Hurry to Beirut
Only to be deafened by the rantings of performance poets.
Spoken words turn the market riotous,
And it's a riot, writing for the market.
Plagiarised melody roars out its rant,
And the sea rolls out a premonition, hints at a rage
That seems, to the fugitive, strange.
All he is fleeing is his witnesses' contempt.
'The honed blades of home' stroke my side
And 'the noose of yearning' fits around my neck,
So I might as well keep pestering that girl made of stone,
Colour in her navel and her breasts
With my brush, and conjure up a Beirutesque kerfuffle!
Taking me up by the scruff of my fright,
She scatters me over the coffee-shops of Rawsha
Like a spray misting from the sea.
If I'm going to sober up, I'd better steer clear of the news-stands
– Their spice is stronger than the dens.
There's no way to slip off the mare
That gallops through the meadow-lands of memory.
I try to be alone with the darkness of the sea.
I sit on the beach, I stretch a foot into the chattering well.
Toes touch the warm fluff of mystery.
Then, at the crossroads of intangible and tangible,
I try to embrace my immortality.
The wine-dark sea is a mirror for those coffee-shops
And sparkles like the necklace that adorns
The ivory throat of Beirut.
I stare in awe at a quart of arak
And the remnants of a stony-hearted scent.
I leave Beirut as I left home, again with a strange premonition:

It'll break out. It's possible.
It'll break out.
They will pitch its tent there.
Yes, its dusty tent will appear.
Its cats will yowl
and spray their eager scent…

With threadbare rags we patch up the holes in the tent.
It's jam-packed with corpses, of course,
Putrefaction piled on putrefaction.
Of the dead, only their halo
Is visible to the faraway viewer;
Resonating, silver as the moon.

That's not the moon. It's a millstone.
And this is War, and it's blind.

It sets forth blithe as a girl
With a come-hither look for the ignorant;
But then it burns its candle at both ends
And ends up a loveless thing, a crone,
Hair cropped, in the dock, detested,
Posing, obscenely, for denouncement.

Do I really care about Baghdad?
The Turkish siege was interminable.
How many heads did it harvest?
Didn't the Tigris monopolise the corpses,
        and take on the scarlet of flags?
The walls would allow in besiegers
        simply to nab them.

Thus the captives multiplied,
And hangings stretched across the Eastern Gate.
It costs so little to stretch
The necks of the lower ranks.

Summer was heavy, heavy...
The dead more fatigued by the sun than the quick.
It takes a stiff arak to fortify the mind
against the slow rot of a rigid daily round
And pickle one till tougher than the grass
They set ablaze with slogans and the flags that come to pass.

I see the women panting after bowls of soup
While young men lap at the wounds of the Almighty,
Then a kid tugs at a soldier's boot
And the clock stands still, tells nothing.

Dulce et decorum est – as they might say
        in the West. The sun hisses
Like wires hiss above flags. Dulce et decorum est.
The sun dries the blood on perished lips.
Dulce et decorum est. Dulce et decorum est.
Dulce et decorum est. Dulce et decorum est.
Dulce et decorum est. Dulce et decorum est.
Dulce et decorum est. Dulce et decorum est.
Dulce et decorum est. Dulce et decorum est.
Dulce et decorum est. Dulce et decorum est.
Dulce et decorum est. Dulce et decorum est.
The kid pulls off the boot of his reclining warrior.
The kid pulls and the neck stretches and so does the rope

And so does the night.

Part Two

My sufferings
    had me in knots from which
My poems kept aloof,
Untainted by the soul's contamination.
Licking my wounds, overwhelmed by farewells,
I became weathered, for sure, but never
Frozen by the ice-blast of suppression.

That froth in the East is the dawn,
Though night allows her skirt to drag
Drunk in a doorway, out of tune;
But won't I insist on discovering
The face of an angel before me
And make excuses for a single slip,
Ignoring a propensity for wantonness?
Haven't I attributed *my* powers to the Tigris
    – not that it's ever noticed –
And sighed, in correspondence with the grass,
Which remains deaf when I sob like a child
    over the dying of flowers?

No point in tarting up nature though,
Nor in revering its negligence.
Is a man scared by a scarecrow?

Countryside, strung on a clothes line.
Dogs kicked out, feral cats
Fossicking in the waste ground
    of downtrodden projects
For what remains of the done-away-with.

The ass in my neighbour's garage
May connect the old way with modernity,
But I can't get out of my head that sardonic glance
Exchanged with the guy the dawn escorted away.
That angel may prove pretty vacant
When questioners tear you apart.

Part Three

He returns to his watering-hole in Baghdad:
Pleasant surprise, lad!
    What you been up to?
How many? How many yielding waves
Have cleaved to his torn sail?
How many landfalls? How many beaches?
Look, it's his hang-out, as for its booze,
He drinks it, affording no answers.
Not any more is the glass some puzzled mouth
Alluding to the wellsprings of a human one,
Nor are its contents blood revealing,
In their unstaunched flow, the murderer's identity,
Nor are the states it induces the wings
    of a boy who flew too high,
Breaking the family mirror.

Ours is a nightspot crashed by a gang.
The waiter finds their faces unfamiliar.
They just barged in, as a house is raided at dawn,
And the corpse of a fellow passing through
    gets thrown out, cold as the rest of them!
Where did they come from?
Who the hell are they?
Where do we go for help?

For fresh air, head for the Tigris. Beside it,
    Gilgamesh is waiting in disguise:
'What happened before will happen again,
And again and again and again,
A fifth and a sixth and a seventh time,
And an eighth and a ninth, it will happen again.

It happens so since the world requires it
        out of regard... for security.
The days of this creature are numbered.
        Its deeds are breaths of air.'
'Yes, but why the modern dress,
        Gilgamesh?'

'The present masks the past
In this long-extant *polis*, where humanity
        dies of a broken heart,
Though the despair that's broken it survives.'
'And what do you suppose will happen now?'
'I look out, over the embankment. I see some corpses floating down,
And me among the corpses.
I know this for certain.
Why? Because the tallest never reach the sky;
And as for the most powerful,
        they cannot hug the earth in its entirety.'
'But what is this embankment?'
'This is the dike that prevents the past from flooding,
        flooding in on us.'

Enkidu's nightmare frightened him to death,
        and yet its signs were false,
As were all his readings.
'Eat the bread, Enkidu, eat it, for this is the staff of life.'
Thus spake the whore of the temple.
'Yes, and drink the wine,
For though it saps your brutishness, it is the custom here.'
And what did he do? He ate, drank and became faint with pleasure.
And didn't it seep into him, the scent of the Euphrates?
And didn't his body then secrete
        a sweat with the palm pollen's odour?
Gilgamesh, don't you remember?
Don't you remember the worms?
Our nightmares frighten us to death, and yet their signs are false.

Then take these streets that creep along like tortoises,
And start, start if you like,
From the start of this street where the bars are.
Go by the sinful bridges and the idiotic lampposts.
Put on a suit, like any of us,
And try our contemporary senses.
You'll not find the sixth, for it rotted away.

Then I woke up on Abu Nuwas Street, just at the start of dawn,
        and the bench was wet, as were all the benches:
The wet, worn benches of each small café.
And wet were the willow groves on sandy, sodden banks nearby,
Wet and rusty were the carved arms of the benches,
        the short arms of the lampposts.
Wet was the smell of the grill
        as the dew dropped down from the night,
And staking out the ground,
Wet were the wooden fences that run between one café and the next,
        Between each bar and the sidewalk;
Fences that wend behind wisteria and hoard the webs of spiders,
These also became wet, and the wetness was an oil on them,
While that odour that gets everywhere,
That odour of inebriated moisture,
        started to waft over Abu Nuwas,
        the cherished street of our secrets.

From a distance you might view the moisture
        lying there slick
        as a mirror in the rain
        that hints at the light's first rays.
A rain that may presage the sun
As waters from the womb announce nativity.

His wet teeth chatter, but the rain silences everything.
Unsullied slickness of asphalt.
A fisherman passes. The drunk,
    shocked by an early awakening,
    rolls off one of the benches:
The reek of its slats is still in his coat-tails today.
A bicycle glides by without a rider,
Then a dog approaches,
Intrigued perhaps by the smell of scraps:
Some dog kicked out, some stray without identity.

I sat up straight on the bench, as the night came to its end.
Then I got up and turned back,
Intent on the other pavement and
The row of stacked, adjoining bars.
I tried to shake the impact of the downpour off my clothes.
Of course, after that, I turned back yet again
For the book and the pad that I'd left on the bench,
Then headed for the Gardenia. It was closed.
No trace there of the stranger, nor of his strange smell.
I placed my forehead on the plate-glass front
And peered in at the darkness of the bar.
And there was nothing there for me to look for.

I couldn't see a single thing I coveted.

Part Four
Seven Poems

1

The waiter sees the mud on my galoshes
And sweat, from a wank, on my brow.
A reek, as from the underwings of bats,
    wafts out, freed from my armpits.
The waiter tries to head me off.
Ah, but the summer urges me
To trample fields not trampled on before
Or take the shape of a beast from another time.
My neighbour grasps my intentions,
Loads them into the chamber of a gun
And fires them off, like rumours,
    before the secret police can apprehend me,
While I fear for my secret. It may be misunderstood,
And so I load my barrel, pretend to blow away my mind…
Lift on an angel's wings
Above a clear horizon – to look down,
Oh, on a home still standing, date-palms, wild and free,
And waters full of fish.

Prepare to land…

But then the waiter heads me off.
Midnight descends
On me and my neighbour.
The bar's fan rotates in eyes and glasses,
Wafting the ashes of numbness over our souls.
Worry-beads dribble, between index and thumb,
    dripping days of bloody deeds,

And the waiter, quite worn down by this routine,
Comes over all bedraggled, like a rat,
While I am the pendulum,
Swung between dreamer and dreams.

Had I got a move on; had I syphoned ink
From the mouths of birds; had I picked a companion
Met on the pavement where you lost
Your footing, pitched your demented
Self into orbit, then we might have met.
I was carrying enough food for both of us:
Bread, dates and oblivion!

Call yourself at home with words!
You'd even give what's just been said the slip,
Hitch yourself to a shooting star
And whirl into orbit, demented, like the greased lightening
You lost so much sleep over, writing it out and then
Rubbing out all you had written,
As if it were written by water on sand or were the script of storms.

3

Brigades are on the move.
The panic of rabbits betrays their approach,
That and the gun-barrel stink, stench of bearded goats
And a bullet's ambush.
All for the sake of a flag
(Again and again, they rupture that virginity
    They stumbled on – reposing in the shade).

But it's kill or be killed, or be killed as one kills:
Bedouin got up as staff laying siege to a land
    whose dried scars disguise
The unstaunched secret of its people.
Uneasily the Bedouin surround
    ashes that seem merely that.
Is the fire smouldering still?
The Kurds come down with the waterfall
And the goats come down with the Kurds.

Look, I'm an Arab in less-than-conventional dress,
And however wary you are,
I share your unease
As I might share your tobacco.
Everyone does well to be on his guard,
Be frightened, brother. I am.

I don't want to spoil your fun, you urges!
Not for me to rein them in, those horses that went wild
And bolted off behind the clouds.
I'll simply go on smouldering
And spread this smoke around.
Let everything go hazy.
Somehow we'll survive.
My generation's had to put up
With its fair share of knocks.
One hid his head inside a shell
And lived below the surface for a while,

Another died within his coat as he tore at his insides
In a country where brigades of fans
Just blow away the dunes,
For what? For nothing. Nothing...
Blown away like spindrift...

'Listen, my friend,'
Says the singer
'What voice other than my own
Ever hoped to please?
I'll go bare-headed under the sun,
Yes, and I'll bask in its charms.'

It's in the light, the city shimmers
Like water, water and palms.

'Look at our love,'
The singer goes on,
'As it sheds its petals
I'll go open-throated.
Glass after glass I'll down,
Drowning our anxious alarms.'

It's in the glass, the city shimmers
Like water, water and palms.

6

We came prepared to weep, my friend and I,
But now we've caught the world with its trousers down
We can't suppress a snigger. Oh, Baghdad,
Baghdad is an out-of-date paper.
Trouble is, the Tigris is illiterate:
Without a clue, it gazes at the pages.
While the palms keep trembling as if terrified
      – blenched, and tatterdemalion as the destitute.
'My friend, take off your shoes.
Take off your shoes and go barefoot,
For this is the last time we tread
The ground of our country.
Tomorrow the footwear of exile will fit us both.'
Never underestimate the Tigris:
It's handed in reports about our bathing bodies.
The wine that we imbibed has betrayed our every confidence,
The moon takes down the dreams in sleeping eyes
And everyone mirrors their fear of each other.
My friend is a double-edged blade.

A convoy trundles down the road to Damascus
The treads of its tyres – our lungs – indent the sand.
Hide your tracks, the night guides say.
Take care! How sweet it is.
How sweet it is when someone disappears.

Disappears:
Exchanges
His clothes for a sash from the sunset,
His memory for some luggage,
His rash for a magic cap,
The convoy for red horses
Racing through the night towards a legend.

Part Five

So let us now praise exodus,
  exodus *en masse,*
Let us now praise exodus before dawn
While checking inside the receiver
  and under the car.
Let us now praise exodus
  as those who are exiled already
  praise those of us who are exiled after them.
Unto them let's advertise our attractions
And publicise our qualities to disbelieving lands.
Our travel songs are shanty towns
  and the sun goes wailing through their slats.
Who dare join their voices to our own?

Let us now praise exodus
  from its first cocoon
  to its children tumbling down the vale.
And let us praise our mourning songs that race us to the sea.
Hallelujah, exodus!
No one's cheered as loud before,
And wandering through us, the slain are on tour.
They pillow their heads on our eulogies,
And, as the light goes out of their eyes,
  we praise that dying light.
Here are roads less stony.
Here we stand, at the summit of Mount Memory.
Our wishes are wolves in the desert:
  scrabbling, scrabbling, never to strike
  the sacred springs of blood,
And the sand soaks up our wishes.

Let us praise the dullness
        that drains all colour out of things,
And, from the lands of the living,
        sing of the lands of the plague.

The Academic's Gown

Serenity is mine, on coming into London,
Where I make my way
    to the great museum's library.
Here the academic's gown soars up as high as the ceiling,
Matched by the tiers around its dome.
'This is no place for physical frailty.'
Down flows the gown – like the flow of decent vintages.
The chill, though, that affects the hand that turns the pages,
And a metal echo to the steps that serve the eyries,
Both of these unsettle me:
'This is no place for a stiffness in the step.'
Unsettled I remain, down the years.

Toccata

I get inside the organ:
    one tunnel after another.
I get in touch with its *djinni*.
It's like I'm holding a girl I happen to love.
She's still intact, and it's only
Her doll's mask face that's gashed
By her garish maroon.
'Can you see my darknesses?' She whispers.
'The smell of decay, the sacks of despair?
Your poetry would shrink a bit,
    were your thirst slaked by mine.'

She slithers about: a toccata,
As I get out wings from the mirror above,
Introduce them with my arms
And hover, like an angel,
Above the organ's holy shrine.

Belonging to Eternity

Do you belong to the shadow of time,
    or does your shadow belong to eternity?
You have to choose.

My skull is a house of clay,
But spring wells up beneath the covered breast,
And somehow a guitar keeps strumming in this tearful heart,
Yet I seem a fisherman becalmed
    somewhere in the marshes of existence.
I have mislaid my nets as well.
But there's not much I can do about it now.
I just tend to dredge up what I can from memory
    and mobilise my finds against the present
Whenever its tightens its noose…
    and threatens me with my shadow.

Family

I am at peace as I enter her mirror
Naked, free of my clothes and of a nagging thought
That got in my way on the way to her.
'You be my clothes,' she says to me,
As the little ones in her arms
Disconcert me with interrogations:

'Dad, you're a bloody old Messiah!
Always on about our going back.
But how long will going back go on for?'

My solace is the wind that drives the flock of clouds.

Part 7

The Dawn Is Near

The grass is covered with dew this Sunday.
I will drink out of the bottle.
A piece of cheese will do me fine.
You only need to light up a pipe to be warm.

No café for me this Sunday.
I will drink out of the bottle until my shirt is damp
And dawn is in the air and the squirrel is alerted to my steps.
Won't a gate swing open in the mist?
'Who are you?' the keepers may demand.
I'll say it's me, the one who writes that metaphysical poetry.
A leaf comes floating down through the mist
And comes to rest on my knee.

This Sunday I left home,
Stepped at last out of my dream and left home.
I walked a path unwalked before; I walked off into a legend.
I can drink out of the bottle, but then I can't hold anything
Together, and I have this urge to sprawl.
I fight against it, though, because the grass is wet
        and because it's very nearly dawn.
Yes, and now that door in the mist swings open.
'Who are you?' they demand.
'Hey, it's me, the one who writes that metaphysical poetry.'
The silence is sour, and remote as some fountain of wool;
My feet are so light they hardly make a sound.
How do I answer the call of the current,
The lure of the palms as they fan out over the river?

I will drink out of the bottle
    until the scent bleeds out of me
    and the soul can be seen through my body.
I will get drunk for a fucked-up country;
Yes, and for a house in Karkh, in the old part,
    hidden from the light of day;
Yes, and for a friend they burnt in a pool of acid,
Or for someone left like a scarecrow
    standing guard over a minefield.
Skulls and fragments of bone,
Wreckage, spoils of war
    given thicker presence by the mud.
You can't get away from the sight of those mouths
    where the breath is stilled.
Is there to be some revivification of their torn bodies?
Is the dawn to be?
Oh, but a piece of cheese will do.
You only need to light up a pipe to be warm.
Anything will do.
So no café this Sunday.

I'll go home... I'll put on the radio.

It's Time to Deepen the Gulf Left by the Roots

It's time to deepen
    the gulf left by the roots.
A tree uprooted grows tall.
Vacating its place of planting,
    it grows, and then it vanishes
Like smoke:
On the water's face
    nothing but the shiver of a breeze.
My friend and I are in a boat.
We lean over and lift the shiver
Off the face of the water,
    making a net of our hands.
The fish quiver, leap and vanish.
I ask: 'Did you see the quiver?
    Did you turn towards the breeze?'
He says: 'I saw. The breeze was chill.
I turned. I heard the sound it made.
How calm the clouds are,
    And how deep the ashes
    that are dissolved in the clouds.'
Then…
Whew, that was close!
Yards away, some buckled chunk of shrapnel
    smashes into the water's face.
Plume of foam.
Reek of smoke.
Fish on their sides on the surface.
Then just another breeze rippling the water.
And the boat panicked.

I said:
      'It could have been a stray shell or a missile.
Somewhere there may be a cannon, or an invisible jet.'
The tree had already gone,
Leaving a gap in the horizon
And there we were, stunned by the impact of its swift retreat.
It's time to deepen
      the gulf left by its roots.

I sat on the seat that spanned the boat
And grabbed the oars, wrenching them against the water as the boat
      sped towards the bank of al-Abbasiyya
I gazed like an idiot into the face of my friend.
He was rendered speechless.
The Jumhouriyya Bridge appeared to the left,
      but just like the tree, it was leaving,
Wrenching up its cement pillars that had their roots in the water,
With a wrenching sound, it was vanishing over the horizon.
Our boat slips in among the row of boats at the wharf.
We leap across to the bank and mount the concrete steps
      in soaking shoes.
From the barrage walk, we look towards our house
And find it rotting by dint of the rain:
Its gutter-spout seems to be missing...

Thirty years go by, and then
      my friend sends me this letter.
Here I am reading it, sitting alone.
The boat gets out for a row still, now and then;
But once a paramilitary speedboat trailed her.
Men with truncheons and riot gear
      boarded her and beat her up.
No use calling for help. She almost sank.

The waters of the Tigris are prohibited.
The smell of fish is prohibited.
Al-Abbasiyya no longer exists.
Its homes were all uprooted and with them the roots of its trees:
    the lotus-tree, the mulberry,
    the eucalypt, the oleander,
    the willow, the joppa,
    the citrus, the palms with their dates...
No shadows left for any secrets.

I didn't reply to his letter, out of caution;
Didn't care to remind him of the buckled chunk of shrapnel
    or the reek of smoke,
Never informed him that I've been arrested by the radio
    and am now a captive of the screen,
Though the fleeing pillars of the bridge
    reappeared before my eyes
Just as I had last seen them,
    lifting out of the disturbed water,
    taking their roots with them,
These are the images.
As for the feelings...

Just let me sink my nails into enemy flesh.
The sheeny skin – just let me make it bleed.

A knock on the door, like the pulse in a vein at the temple,
    discovers my head in my mother's deepest folds,
    her darkest and her warmest folds.
A knock on the door,
And I slip from the folds to be picked up by a passer-by.
The door is smashed by the knocking, and I go to pieces.

A knock on the door,
    and the shaking it causes teaches me my identity.
A knock on the door, and I go up in smoke.
A knock on the door, and I switch tracks,
    escaping into the strangeness of strange lands,
And, as the knocks go on and on,
    I find no way of shutting them out,
And again
There's a knock on the door.

The grass is covered with dew this Sunday.
I will drink out of the bottle.
A piece of cheese will do me fine.
You only need to light up a pipe to be warm.

I am taken aback, as it stretches before me.
Before they layed down the asphalt,
    it was like sandpaper sheets, this bridge,
Because of its fine, pale flagstones
    and the pallid glow from its lamps.
Known as the Queen Aliya Bridge, it became, after the Revolution,
    the Bridge of the Republic.
I start across its asphalt,
    barefoot, I start across;
    get halfway and retrace my steps.
All my excitement has been wrenched out of me.
From its steps, I reach the ground that moves like a magic carpet
Towards the house; past the dignity of our serene parliament,
And, since the river's in view, I can fish out the swimmers from here.
I can extract the silt that plugs their navels;
    the Babylonian silt.

I can extract the scent of hemp;
    the lines that follow the carp into the depths of the current.
'A giant fish the size of a ghoul,' cries Ahmed al-'Isa.
Naked men stand straight
On their legs like storks, jabbing with their eyes
    at the holes of a sinking net.
I'm practically the offspring of the palm-shoots.
These we slit with our razors
    to get to the scent at their hearts.
Ouf, there's a stench to the plot instead!
Shock of something smouldering, and scorched.
I grip my robes in my teeth and take off.
The wing of a hostile jet
    smacks against the horizon.
I take evasive action, dodge and scream, the bridge, the bridge!
Vertiginous lamp-posts set up a whine,
Wattle-and-daub huts fill with lamentations.
As is his wont, my father gets in around supper time,
    wearing his oil-stained suit.
Having moored his dinghy on the rocks,
He's come home worn out.
My father has been working on the bridge.
'Today a man fell,' he tells us.
    'Landed in the pillar's mesh guts.
Didn't have time to draw breath.
The mixer tipped and covered him quick
With the next load of cement.
A bridge has to have its sacrifice, I suppose.'
It only happened once.
There was no substance to the other allegations.
My father weighed it all up.
You had to face it:
    some just die of bad luck.

As for those who die from bad assumptions,
He didn't know about that. How could he,
Dying, as he did, before the worst of it?
Before our noble parliament became a mere assembly,
And before our street became
        a hotbed of informants... or patriots.
Whinings and lamentations merge into one wail,
And my voice gets lost in the wail, and my being's hid
        By the screen of smoke
        the jets left as they bombed,
            howling like a pack of wolves as they harried down on us...

...Just as Christ stretches,
Baghdad emerges,
        horribly stretched, with both hands nailed.
Baghdad accompanies my wailing:
'O country of thirst
        and trees beyond thirst!'
Baghdad hides her bleeding, out of timorousness.
Baghdad drags her once-proud skirts
And wanders along a beach at sunset.
Baghdad is an ashtray for the residue of bullets,
Yet she is keen to be saved,
So why are the soldiers retreating?
Why does the water flow away
Along with the proudest of horses?

Why does the grip of two rivers prove so perplexing?
Why does the tossing of the palms exhaust me?
Because the village domes
        would launch now into space
            ...migrating with the storks;

And I, I shall go with them,
Lift off, out of the thickets, leave the grass behind,
And follow the domes, in their airy, blue rotundity,
My flight taking me
        higher and higher,
Just like a tree growing up,
        growing further
        and further away from the day of its planting,
Vanishing upwards like smoke,
And at the faint blue margin of its vanishing
I'll come across God looking terribly Arab;
His beard adrip with tears.

I am taken aback, as it stretches before me.
Before they layed down the asphalt,
        it was like sandpaper sheets, this bridge,
Because of its fine, pale flagstones
        and the pallid glow from its lamps.
I have my new poem with me
        and brandish my allegiance to the 60s:
I'm practically the offspring of the palm shoots.
These we slit with our razors
        to get to the scent at their hearts…

The café set confound me with their confidences:
Everybody getting out their handkerchiefs
        – like butterflies that flutter over tables.
We are, for sure, the offspring of the shoots:
The scent from our hearts competing with others
In the knot of smells:

the tang of tea, of coffee beans,
of dry lemon, cinnamon, hash,
arak, naphthalene, damp straw mats,
mud, and dust, and the smell of the sun,
reek of turning fans… and fear,
odour of transcendent souls,
books and slippers, sperm that's been ejected,
together with the gases of the drowned,
slipping away down the current of our griefs.
At the Hassan al-Ajmi café,
Al-Baladiyya café, al-Samar,
Zuhair, al-Mu'aqqadin, Ra'ad, Yasin, al-Parliament,
Um Kalthoum and al-Imyan, we worry at the knot of smells.

I mingle with the crowd.
The air is hot and the walkers are aimless.
I drift from Bab al-Mu'adhem toward al-Maydan Square
On the same side as the Ministry of Defence.
Grubby paper aeroplanes
    are floating
        down
            towards the pavement.
And, in al-Maydan Square, sitting at the Bar al-Baladiyya,
I come to share an unexpected destiny
    with this crowd that wallows in illusion:
Generation haunted by a shot, knifed by a shadow,
    threatened by the States
    now – as grubby jets missile-blast that Ministry.
So much for defence! I cough,
Splattered in the aisles of the al-Jumhouri hospital.

'The Zaïm's dead,' it's rumoured,
Even if his contented face can still be seen on TV.
The Ba'thists got him, dragged his corpse
        by the feet and tied it to a chair
        – peppered through with holes –
'Here he is!' they said.
My mother cried, as she gripped my arm,
And I began to cry as well,
Because of the turmeric tincture to her wrinkles.

I'm so ashamed:
        for I hold in my arms
        a country on the brink of disaster:
Its violated cities,
And its refugees
        pausing on the bridge,
        hawking up their guts –
'And its stately palm with its elongated fronds –
        assuredly the master of all trees,'
And its oleander, daughter of the clay,
And the holy shrines of its broken-hearted mother,
And its young whose promise has been drowned,
And all the wandering coats and voices
        screaming in its dens…
In Iraq's interminable night.
I'm so ashamed
        of what I hold in my arms,
        although I know my burden's Mother Earth.

The war broke out at dawn on the 17th of January:
The sky-line was as grey as it can be,
Though a sweet breeze from Araby
        blew across the minefields…

...soldiers, jungle stalkers, cats,
They all sink their claws in tender flesh.
Lit cigarettes
        gleam like the eyes of an ogress.
The camel-driver accompanies an insouciant flock to the site.
And the insects that fall on their backs in the dark
Seem as confused as the mercury in the thermometer.
An oven glows in the tent, and the wind miaows and sinks in
        its teeth and its claws,
            and the body moans and bleeds.

...Baghdad

It's all twinkling like a Christmas tree!
The screen is just too small to show the impact.

There was a heavy dew when I left home.
I stepped at last out of my dream
To see the rays of a humid dawn
        put halos round your every dome, Baghdad.
I saw the birds of your enemies
        attack and lacerate those rays,
I saw the debris of the dead...

Baghdad is a moaning in the tunnel of eternity.
Baghdad is a flag, handed on by forgotten corpses.
Baghdad is a book a ghost might read on a really lonely night.
Baghdad mirrors the mask of the killer.

This Sunday I left home,
Stepped at last out of my dream and left home.

Ah, but I am sick of your normality,
And of your damp democracy, and of your foggy flowers,
Normality of City gents and aluminium eyes,
Sick of the stock market of your desires,
Sick of your self-esteem…

I am obsessed by the alleys between stacked dwellings
        in a neglected land,
Obsessed by the mud on the foot of a boy,
Obsessed by the shards of corpses fluttering like blackened angels,
And by my good intentions and… by the touch of your glove.

How lonely one's shadow is as it approaches
The bulk of your shadow, opera house,
Where I must shut my ears to that *bel canto,*
Calming an ageing morning and a night congealed.
I am obsessed by the hot sun of my homeland,
And by its sombre night,
And by its water seething with fish.
How lonely one's shadow is as it approaches your shadow!

This Sunday I left home,
Stepped at last out …of illusions… into your mirrors.
The grass is covered with dew.
A piece of cheese will do.
You only need to light up a pipe to be warm.

No café today… and I will not return.

The Last Song

I shall come back
To say, 'I'm drunk on idleness,'
To breathe the scent of rain-dripped walls
And watch the restless sunflower's growth.
I shall come back
To say, 'I'm drunk on the shade
Of the mulberries that overhang our glasses.'
I shall come back
To sing of those who drank with me.
And it is enough
To mourn my father's house;
To mourn for us – who abandoned it –
And, for the slain,
A shadow is enough;
As a frightened shadow's kohl-touched look
Is enough to feed the ache
Of those Iraqis who forget to ache;
Those who will never come back;
To say, 'It's here,
The hillside where my growing-up expressed itself.'
And it is enough to express my impatience...
Everything in ruins...
I shall come back
To sink my nails in your sorrows,
Use your silt to stain my hands
And say, 'I'm drunk on your bitter
    Baghdad coffee.'
I can be drunk on hope as well...
    ...once in a while.

A Reader in Darkness

Before you go to bed you insist on switching the lights off
And checking, by touch, in the darkness, that you locked the door
And that you pulled down the blinds.
You leap like a cat up the stairs
And slip into your bed,
And dream –

That the book you were reading at your desk
Is being opened again in the darkness:
Other fingers are turning its pages;
Other eyes rest their gaze
On the absence that repeats between the lines…

A Soldier

Hundreds of scarf-swathed soldiers
Pass through our applause
As through a cave there passes a draught of cold air.
We hardly know them, and yet they acknowledge our tributes;
Dishevelled, rusted for ages, barefoot.
They have woven a history like a fishing-net
Which has unravelled in stagnant water.
The rust has encrusted their fingers and furred their elbows.

My house is a stack of those moments
That are defined by books, papers and paintings.
A single touch can disrupt it all.
Sometimes a breeze approaches,
At others though a soldier comes across.

At the Gardenia's Entrance

In front of the Gardenia's bolted entrance,
A middle-aged man with the look of someone who has retired
    is waiting.
I am also a middle-aged man, just returned from exile.
I squat a few feet from him,
And without wasting much time, I ask:
    'Do you know when it opens?'
'The Gardenia Bar was my hangout before the war.
I used to have my own corner there
    with my friends around me.
After the war, it folded, got forgotten.
But I have been coming here for a long time
    waiting each day for its door to open.'

He stretched a hand out, holding a rolled cigarette,
And I stretched a hand to take it
And smoke spread, blurring the two men
    waiting at the bolted door
On the sidewalk of Abu Nuwas Street.

Silent Nature

In the yard
A rusted tap
Underneath a flowering oleander.
Behind the oleander is a door.
It's occupied now by a doubtful shadow.
The shadow counts the drops as they fall
Into a stagnant pool.
                      In the house
The sun is unique,
Radiant as the scales of some dead fish;
And the tight oleander flowers
Seem like the nipples of a pregnant woman
Thrusting in the crisis of her labour.
How dark the green of this oleander branch!
How dusky this oleander scent!
And the tart glue on the flowers,
Oh, how seductive it is, in the sun,
For all the flies of the house.

Letters

Why is it only me who writes letters every month?
I try to respond to your silence,
Pretending that your silence is more eloquent
Than my words.
Every month I add to your name
All that I love of your traits:
Dear lady of longing, dear jasmine,
    and dear flowers that encircle gardens
Till my windowpane has gathered
    from a mouth its dew of vapour.
Sighs of the lady of longing?
But it was night, breaths of cold night wind.

And so I finish my letter.
And after thirty days I try to respond to your silence again,
Pretending that your silence is more eloquent
Than my words.

On one side, my always departing letters;
On the other side, your silence,
And between them
The earth and the sun keep rotating.
Whole histories are chronicled in the names of these two,
The one in writing and the other in silence,
While empires rise and fall.

The Cold Sculpture

All year the vine
Encroaches on my home
Without putting forth
A single leaf.

Its roots run deep
Through the loam
Sustaining its dark fingers.

Me, I go unbound,
Knowing poetry may come about
Without sound,
Without ink or paper.

Under repetitive murmurs
I can sense words unspoken:
Feeling such awareness
Is a drunkenness.

Clothing amounts
To my port in a storm,
Though my destination
Is nowhere.

Me, this isolate sculpture.
I'm cold.
My plinth is the void.

The River

Three poems about the river Tigris

1
The Cliff

The waves wash back from the bank,
And there's my father's shadow in his skiff,
And there's a vein like the veins of a hand
Fossilised in the familiar cliff.
There's green pottery, seals, and a mud tablet,
Villages blurred by their moss,
And a muted voice in the conches
Booming about the hoof-beats of the unknown.
Echoes vibrate in a shell…
And the waves swing back to wash against the bank.

2
A Vision

Both of them are concerned
And cautious of course:
'Would you like to drink a toast for those who've disappeared,
Karim Minor?'
'Come, I've had enough of all their lies...'
And so they leave.

I see them like the summer's scent over water,
Raising a throne for the night of the body.
I see the fronds like diadems on their foreheads,
And mulberry branches tied around their waists.
I stretch my hands out:
This is my youth,
        or delusion...
        or memory's clamour.

I see them, like the shrines around a fireplace,
And I hear their voices like candles afloat on the waves,
Sending their trembling longing to me...
And sleep overwhelms:

(What has remained
Of the Tigris except for the burning of roots,
The mouth of an abyss
And a warning voice that roars,
'Water and the drowned
Water and the drowned
Water and the drowned...')

3
Or Because I Am Far Away

If I were not a desire – like your waves that never settle,
Or an apparition, behind the veil, on both of your banks,
What else could I be?
And you, Tigris, as you have always been my father's domicile
And my protection against strangers,
Why do I presume that your waterway is a symbol
    invented by others
And that your Babylonian alluvium is false evidence
And your voice pure fabrication?
Is it for fear of finding a waterway narrower than I remember?

Dust... dust
And the glass turns upside down.
Is there a voice behind the wall?
And does the poem therefore slip from my hand?
Or is it because I am so far away
I only catch the echo of myself:
No more than a rumour of a distant land?

Emigrant Convoys

I don't take in the prose of Abu Hayyan
In the boozy hour of its company, as I get through a night alone,
But dwell upon my journey in the convoy of the emigrants:
That never-ending jolting between continents.
And I recall the faces of the emigrants.
How shocked I was by their masks, by their deceits.

Before I retire to bed,
I hear the dark's custodian
Saying, 'What unmasks the mask
Is the smile it spreads in sleep
(And here Sleep smiled to himself).

And I have seen the Devil in his mask
Smile at those who sleep beyond midday.
Seen, in the glint of night, his grin
Feed on the effulgence of the stars.

After that experience in the wilderness,
I touch my mother's dress – a time not mine –
Trace in my father's palm the line that leads to oblivion.
Everyone I see reveals his present time   .
As a wish for a few grains of sand
To seed the thread of his past, that line
Embedded, entrapped in his hands.

History! Who does it care about, other than us?
We are the builders of ephemeral cities
Dedicated solely to its chronicles.

What does it care for the earth's rotation
Compared to our circling steps?

This handful of words on the gravestones of the lost.
When should the skilled hand incise them
If not in a war?

I see the emigrant convoy
Take a turn now that was never mine,
And just before it disappears, it glitters
Like the pendant of some puzzled star.

The Last Gypsies

The grey has got into our hair
And the wind no longer weaves our braids.
Our horses have put on weight
    and the dead have become our shrines.
Whenever the wind from the hills swoops down on us,
Don't we squeak like hollow bones?

No wolf dares to eye the face of the night in us,
Nor does the sun dare enter our wells.
Yet ever, when you look, you find there are more of us.

You, who avoid coming close,
We would advise you to tremble.
Although you see in our cities ruins and skeletons,
We are not victims of some past epidemic
Nor were we ever fodder for lost wars.

No, we are your mirrors.

We trek across the distance without pursuing a clue,
Without being fixed on some glory interred in the ruins.
Yet still we cherish hopes of our addressing you
With mouths that may win our demands down the years
And blood that longs for the West.
This is why we watch the horizon
And follow the course of the sun until it sets.

This is home, oh housebound ones:
A body forever in transit,
    heavy with the taste of tears.

The Voice of Inner Life

As I go picking berries, or choosing a book
From the shelf; as I enjoy the odour of markets,
Or sense on my face, on a summer's night,
The balm of the mid-river breeze,
Or lie on a camp-bed up on our roof,
        overwhelmed by the moonlight,
Or feel the henna charm my hip,
        beneath the *punka* of our neighbour's palm,
Or a minor mood takes over – but what for? –
Or as I brave the mole caught up in storms,

I know you're there, pure voice of inner life.
At night, I try to still my tongue with a glass,
Put away my reams of verse, in order for you to speak.

The Dissident Student

For many years he listens to me
As the trees will listen to the seasons.
In my wake, he wades against the flow,
Getting to the source.
Yes, but the truth is, he never lets up,
Even wrecks my siesta,
Dictating through my tired mouth the most confusing gibberish,
Though he's forever mindful, as if holding back.

One day, when I'm getting on in years,
Flashing like some diamond, he bursts in on me,
Spins me out of my turban,
Throws my ink and papers in my face
And takes off for his rendezvous with fate.

Ever since, people console me.
And it's my wont to indulge them,
Though without any conviction;
For even now, indeed ever since
He brought about the destruction of my perch,
I see in his departing prints
A path for wisdom beyond my commendable inkpot.

Frogs

Leaping out in the rain,
Well-camouflaged:
Blue and then green

In splashes, craters unfurling
Like parachutes
Around them;

Bursting and then folding,
And lit up at times
By the lightning.

Me, I was out in the rain
In the rags of a scavenger,
Searching for words

Which interrupt life
Just as the croaking of frogs
Overwhelms the hiss of the rain.

The Invaders

At night I switch off every light,
Leave the windows free of curtains,
And open the doors wide.
I display for the invaders:
Books, inkpots, and ghosts exchanging toasts.
I drag the train of my royal robe
Followed by twinkles of stars up the stairs
Without guards and doorkeepers.

Ascending, I witness the removal of the veil
And select from the net of the galaxy
What fits me in order to vanish
Into its enticing night.

The Scent of Mulberry

Which one of us knows to whom we belong:
We to you, with this our wrinkled face?
Or you to us, who favour roads of no-return?
Or do both of us, O Baghdad, belong to the hangman?

The scent of mulberry clings to my sleeves,
But the mulberry has long since disappeared,
And the fish no longer penetrate the current.
Both began flowing down, like rivers, to the sea.

Who can earn tomorrow's sustenance
From the memory of a soil fertilised by corpses?
And who can triumph in a wanderlust that is against his nature?

Between the world of nightmare
And the world of water and shade,
Only our poems hang here – like barriers of barbed wire.

History

The steward of my fortress
Informs me: 'O my Master,
You have had enough
Of meat, wine and sleep.
Truly, you're the master
Of that mortal affliction a body:

Like mercury, your soul
Slips through your hands.
The roots of all desires
Have shrivelled up, their water
Has run dry – the sand
Is unyielding. Master,
        you have had enough.'

The time of sand is infinite.
Endless!
        Infinite is the sand.
It runs out now
        With no letting up,
No pause to see
        or to breathe.
No space at all,

O steward of my fortress.

What Was My Choice?

1

You have learned to allow a tiny space
    in the head for any contingency.
Yet, losses, losses come suddenly
– Of the river, and of the palms that hung in the balance,
And among that crescent of friends that used to circle your glass.

Then in one moment you peel yourself away from your love
And alone, dim-sighted, grope your slow way home,
The light of the street lamps heavier than darkness,
The burden of exile heavier than memory.

Tantalising ourselves with hope
Shielding ourselves against… ah, but the question in the guts
Of exiles suddenly attacks:
– What, just what have you chosen?

No longer trusting ourselves
Not to betray the spirit
By being absorbed into the spirit of God,
We watch for the snares of others
As if we were tripwires in ourselves.

2

Exile took us by surprise:
A surgeon ready-scrubbed,
He treated us with scalpels,
Cleansed us of the dream tumours in our organs,
And pushed us into the last scene of the shadow theatre
In order that we perform for him our secondary roles.

Who are we?

Fury of some blind old man
        led by the thread of his loss:
Dice thrown on the night's page,
        leaving not an echo of their rolling.

Give Me this Day my Daily Bread

Give me this day my daily bread
And give me the wish
To negotiate the carnage
Strewn across the road to you.

Lord,
I stand alone before you
Taking my last supper.
I follow a train of ants
To the cold remains
Of the words upon my table.

Just as the meat
Keeps the cold from my bones,
Let this incantation
Afford my ears a bastion.

For if I am at one with the rhythm
Of the spheres' rotation, Lord,
I grasp each passing increment
As time takes flight across my palm;
Jealously guarding my depths,
Miserly with this void
Which confers silence to words.

My eyelashes induce the sun to set
As I reach for another dawn
In my existence,
Turning as the spindle of our turning world,
The centre of some infinite circle.

Four Variations and a Coda

Let each of us tread a path
And brush out the footprints
So as not to leave a trace
        for the days to hound him down.
But whoever accompanies the self will be disturbed by anguish.
Therefore I am cautious about being with myself.

For years I've been addicted to a mask.
I scented in the body the smell of a dragon.
I mated the adversaries in my being
        and left them to it.
I have no companions but the clouds scattered by the winds
Or the dune or the priest
        at the edge of his desires
Or absence as a thing in itself.

I can access the self, if I abstract the self from all chronicles,
And I've built a lighthouse in an everlasting night
There I reside – and await,
        without consolation, what will not arrive.

Someone may tread a road by himself
And brush out the footprints
So as not to leave a trace for the days to hound him down;
But halfway along the way back
He will encounter a different human form
        that is his other side,
And there they will unite and be complete.

A Marble Woman

For twenty years,
I have been observing a shadow pairing of speech and stone
As the poem takes the shape of a marble woman
In the midst of an orchard,
Exposing exquisite lines to the sun.

The more nature grants me of its wisdom,
The more attentive I am to the core of darkness:
To swift claws at my temples,
To the smell
Rapidly diffusing the contaminating touch.

I therefore observe, in the field of my verse,
How the marble appears, in the night,
As a shadow of meaning.
Later one senses the bones, and there comes about
An articulate warmth: the ultimate promise of speech.

Afterword and Notes on the Poems

Swimming in the Tigris, Greenford
The Poetical Journey of Fawzi Karim

Greenford is not where one might expect to find one of Iraq's most esteemed poets, and, in truth, I'd never quite registered the place. The likelihood of my going to Baghdad was just a bit less remote than of my ever finding reason to go to Greenford although I *have* been to Perivale. Young Poles have largely taken it over, such that 'Green*fort*' is spoken of in Katowice, and even Gliwice, as a borough of promise. Although it sounds, and looks, like a modern suburb, it is first mentioned in a Saxon charter of AD 845 as 'Grenan Forda' and almost 200 years later it appears, verbally congealed, in the Domesday Book with a named population of twenty-seven people *and one Frenchman*. There were no Poles. An Iraqi was unthinkable. Another interesting thing about Greenford is that its Tube station is the only one in London to have an escalator going from street level to platform level and it is also the last escalator to be made of wood. The others were replaced with steel in the wake of the King's Cross fire. True to its name, Greenford boasts expanses of green across which I saw not a soul move.

Greenford, Middlesex. It slipped into one of John Betjeman's verses.

I first met Fawzi Karim at a party in Kensington for a New York writer who is legendary for emptying the contents of other people's refrigerators, as he did mine once. Also, when bored, which is often, he flings his hearing aid on the dinner table. The party, all in all, was not such a bad one. I was enthusiastically introduced to Fawzi by the poet Anthony Howell, co-translator of his long poem *Plague Lands*, which shall here serve as a template for his life. We spoke for ten minutes, maybe more, and although this was over a year ago, when it came time for me to seek out an Iraqi for my world journey through London it was Fawzi who first came to mind. Something about him had greatly struck me, which may have been the quietude of one in whom exquisite manners blots out the boorishness of barbaric times. (I might have said 'civilised values' but as of late the term has been hijacked by besuited savages.) And there was something, too, about Fawzi's quiet, slightly gravelly, voice, which could be heard above the world's noise. It was quite without pressure. Also, although this did not unduly influence me, he made kind remarks about a series of articles I'd written on Damascus, a city he knows well and which, on occasion, stands in for the city he is not able to return to.

I arrived at his home in Greenford just as a Bach toccata was coming to a close. One wall of his living room is shelved with CDs of classical music, including almost every opera in existence. Fawzi, as I would soon discover, is one of the very few Arab authorities on Western classical music. Also, there is an ancient wind-up HMV gramophone with a golden horn, similar to the one that was in his family home in Baghdad. Fawzi told me how, as a child, he listened endlessly to an old 78 of the Egyptian singer, Mohamed Abdel Wahab, and memorised the lyrics, repeating one line over and over, little realising he was duplicating a skip on the record's surface. There are a good many books, many of them biographies of composers, and poetry, of course, in English and Arabic. And then there are the oil paintings that serve to demonstrate Fawzi might equally be considered an artist. But then, why not *both*? Why not get over this Anglo-Saxon prejudice of allowing people only a single vocation in life? The paintings are, in spirit and theme, perfectly aligned with his poems, and indeed Fawzi speaks of the paintings collectively as 'a poet's mirror'.

One canvas in particular haunts me.

The poet swims naked in the Tigris, the same age he was when he did the painting, in his late fifties. Fawzi, though, has not, at least in the physical universe, swum in those waters since his early teens. The image, even before one learns this, is dreamlike.

'The sense I get is that the Tigris, even more so than the city it divides, is the great force behind your poetry. Correct me if I'm wrong, but it would appear it also flows through London.'

A serious man, Fawzi laughs only when he means to.

'It may run even stronger here than at its source in Turkey because it belongs to memory rather than to reality which belongs to time that is completely gone. An important thing to remember about Iraq is that when dealing with memory and experience most people there belong to small, enclosed areas and not to the country as a whole. I grew up in Karkh area of Baghdad which is on the west side of the Tigris. My actual district was al–Abbasiyya, which is now completely gone. It was destroyed in order to make way for Saddam's palace gardens. It was a beautiful area, natural and simple, full of palm trees. Many of its inhabitants were poor, their livelihood dependant on fishing, farming and dates. We would climb those palm trees, and the smell of the dates when they were not yet ripe, a stage that in Arabic is called *kimri*, was like human semen, a smell that still reminds me of growing into adulthood. The ancient Egyptians regarded the palm tree as a fertility symbol and from ancient times Iraqis have believed that palm trees contain souls. There is even a legend of someone cutting into the crown of a palm and hearing a high voice coming from inside. Nobody would ever dream of cutting down one of those trees, although during the war with Iran many hundreds of thousands were lost. There was an island in the middle of Tigris, which we'd cross over to in our boats. We would plant things there. We built temporary houses with *hasir*, which is made from reeds. The young people spent their nights there. I spent much of my childhood fishing and swimming in the river. Later, because it was too close to the palace, Saddam banned all boats and even swimming was forbidden. I had no experience of the river as a whole, only of the half kilometre or so which belonged to our area. At the same time, this water was a mythical thing that belonged to Sumerian civilisation. Myth cancels or diminishes the idea of time, so that you find yourself living in the same dimension as the Sumerians. That's why in *Plague Lands* Gilgamesh and Enkidu are actually *there*.'

'The Tigris will nudge us with its epics,' writes Fawzi. Several pages later in the poem, Gilgamesh appears beside the river in disguise. 'What happened before will happen again,' he says, to which the authorial voice in the poem replies, 'Yes, but why the modern dress, Gilgamesh?' Gilgamesh, looking over the embankment, sees corpses floating down the river, his own among them. Another image that appears early on in the poem relates to the ancient Iraqi custom of placing lit candles on plates made from rushes and floating them down the river in celebration of that most mysterious figure of religion and folklore, al-Khidr, a Muslim saint whose Christian and Jewish counterparts are St George and Elijah, and whose mythic origins may in fact pre-date all three religions. It had been my intention once to pursue the subject of al-Khidr through the minds of the people who most revere him. It was a pleasant surprise to meet him again in Fawzi's poem. As a figure who might serve to make all three religions tolerable to each other, there is none more appropriate.

'I put a certain light on it now, of course, but I recognised that mythical dimension even at a very early age. Sometimes you understand things without language, as a kind of music inside you, which only much later becomes words. All that I have, even my relationship with the Book, has its origins in al-Abbasiyya. We had a Shi'a mosque there called Hussainiyya, which I belonged to because of its library. As a young boy I became manager of that library. So I began there, with the Word and the Book, although not really with the information contained in those books, and even now I feel some separation between words and their meaning. I loved and collected books, often reading from them in my high voice. The Arabic books, especially the old ones, came mostly from Beirut and Cairo, and had uncut pages which one had to open with a knife. You could smell things rising from their pages. I could smell the shapes of words as they rose, and even their meanings had their own shapes. There was no separation, no paradox, between things. When later, insensitive to the religious atmosphere, I introduced volumes of modern poetry and prose, some of it quite irreligious, I was asked to leave.'

There is a paradox which remains at the very root of Fawzi's thinking. One needs first to understand the layout of a typical Arabic home, the greater part of which is hidden from public view. Its rooms surround an open space, a small garden paradise suggestive of the greater Paradise that awaits those of high moral virtue.

'When I was a child we had two trees in the courtyard of our house. There was the mulberry which was full of light, beneath whose spreading branches my aunt who was blind took shelter from the sun. I used to climb up between the leaves, and there the light flooded in from all directions. The other was the oleander which was the mulberry's extreme opposite, a dim and closed tree, which never accepted our human presence. Its sap was bitter to the taste, sticky, and attracted flies. I like both these trees, but to which do I belong, the mulberry or the oleander? One is bright and open and extroverted, while the other absorbs the light and keeps it there. Although the worlds they represent are for me totally separate, I feel I belong to both of them. I think I prefer the first one, but it's the second which pulls me more. When I speak about music and literature, the difference, say, between Tolstoy and Dostoevsky, or Hemingway and Kafka, often I think of those two trees. Dostoevsky is the oleander because his dark journey is contained *there*. Among painters, the Expressionists belong to the oleander, unlike the Impressionists who belong to the mulberry, who go outside to play amid colour and light. When I listen to Bizet's *Carmen*, I am again reminded of my relationship with those trees. Don José falls in love with Carmen while at the same time he still loves this angelic girl. I think he feels guilty when he leaves Micaëla for Carmen but this guilt pushes him even more to love this dark woman. This is exactly my struggle. I do not *like* the oleander – nobody can like it – so why am I obsessed by this dark, secretive tree, even though as a boy I belonged, body and soul, to the mulberry? Always there are these two directions between which I can't choose. That's why from the very beginning I felt it was impossible to believe, either religiously or ideologically, in any one thing. I am divided on the inside. While I may have been a Marxist once, as an ideology I knew Marxism was impossible. I can appreciate Plato's *Republic* as a great work of imagination but to make this republic real would be to create a hell for people. I think my poems reflect this inner struggle or what the painter Kandinsky calls "the inner necessity".'

We would salute that oleander, hot with our uniqueness.

That oleander of Fawzi's childhood, whose shoots so often take root in his verse, was chopped down for firewood. This was when Saddam's henchmen took over and destroyed people's houses in order to make room for his palace. When Fawzi said the oleander's sap was bitter to the taste, I wondered *whose* taste. The oleander contains toxic compounds, including cardiac glycosides, only a small dose of which can cause the heart to race and then dramatically slow down, often with fatal consequences. There is no part of the plant that does not contain a deadly poison, and its poisons are various. A single leaf can kill a child, and the bark contains rosagenin which produces effects not dissimilar to those caused by strychnine. The seeds may be ground up and, as has been the case in southern India, used for purposes of suicide. A small amount of sticky white sap causes the central nervous system to collapse, with resultant seizures and coma. What is especially poignant here is that its burning wood produces highly toxic fumes, which, as a symbol for a country in flames, could hardly be more apposite.

'When I think back on my childhood on the Tigris, I realise there were all these great benefits. All the symbols became real, full of life and mythology. It is a river that continues to run through my poetry. I realised later that poetry does not deal with history but with myth, which is why I criticise most Arabic poets because they respond mostly to current events. This is not their job. Poetry deals with something else. A poet has to neglect historical time and go beyond it.'

Maybe what makes this image so arresting is its perspective. Fawzi, seven years old, stares not into ours but into his own distance. It's as if everything in the photograph is set to his gaze. It is 1952, presumably winter – well, cool enough for him to be wearing a coat – and he is returning home from the school which, so I am told, is hidden somewhere in the shadows behind him. A smudge behind the vehicle, as if the ghost of some greyer architecture, is the old parliament building, which later was replaced by the National Assembly, and it will be on the road from there, six years hence, that Fawzi will see something terrible, which will direct the course of his life. The ditch filled with water – there is another hidden from view on the opposite side of the road – belongs to the ancient irrigation system that channels water directly from the Tigris to the gardens of the houses. Water is, for obvious reasons, a dominant theme in Arabic literature but worth noting is a famous hadith in which the Prophet Muhammad says one should never waste water even when sitting beside a river. One of the buildings to our left of Fawzi is the local café. A bit deeper into the future, when Fawzi is seventeen and already plagued with verses, its owner will doubly, triply wipe the tea glasses clean, and, soon after, even break them, because the lips that touched them were those of an Unbeliever; that is, if we are to equate a poet asking questions about existence with atheism.

What is even more interesting, and I mean no disrespect to our subject, is the ewe a few yards behind him. It belongs to a woman who lived in one of the houses nearby. The ewe is called *Sakhlat al-'Alawiyya* which translates, somewhat clumsily, as 'the sheep of the woman of the family of the Imam 'Ali', and because it is so illustriously connected it is considered a sacred creature, which may go wherever it likes, whether it be into shops or houses, and almost always with a treat in store. Ill fortune comes to anyone careless enough to shoo it away. Fifty years later, a childhood friend of Fawzi's, looking at this photograph, will remark, 'Why, this is the ewe of the holy woman!' There is nobody of that time and place who doesn't know that creature. What the photo represents for Fawzi is not just a lost world but also, in the relationship between the ewe and the people among whom it so freely moves, forever safe from the butcher's knife, a metaphysical one. It is a world in which a nearby lotus-tree is believed to harbour a djinn that at night throws stones at people who come too close. It is a world of mystery and between it and its inhabitants there is an easy correspondence. Such questions as will be asked are the poet's prerogative. The boy would already appear to know this. The ewe certainly does.

*

There are some people whose lives may be read as narratives, and others, Fawzi's among them, whose lives can be seen as clusters of images. A Caesar demands a narrative; a Virgil is all images. We began with Fawzi swimming in the ancient waters of the Tigris.

What is a river, though, without its bridge? A bridge is one of the most potent of images. It can symbolise a link between the perceptible and the imperceptible, a connection between direct opposites, or it can represent a transition from one world to another, or, with its destruction, a sundering between them. In 1952, when Fawzi was seven, his father worked on the construction of the nearby Queen Aliya Bridge, which, after the Revolution of 1958, was renamed the Jumhouriyya Bridge or 'The Bridge of the Republic'. There Fawzi would take his father picnics in the three-tiered container that has a Turkish rather than Arabic name: *safartas*. Fond though those memories are, they also contain an incident responsible for one of several violent passages in Fawzi's poem, all the more terrifying for being presented in a flat conversational tone.

My father has been working on the bridge.
'Today a man fell,' he tells us.
    'Landed in the pillar's mesh guts.
Didn't have time to draw breath.
The mixer tipped and covered him quick
With the next load of cement.
A bridge has to have its sacrifice, I suppose.'

Those lines seem to connect to the construction, between 1931 and 1932, of the White Sea-Baltic Sea Canal, when approximately 100,000 Gulag prisoners perished, their bodies used as fill by their Soviet masters who, much to Comrade Stalin's pleasure, completed the work four months ahead of schedule.

'This bridge became an important symbol in my writing. I was from a small, unknown area, and when, aged sixteen, I started publishing my first poems in magazines, nobody knew where I was from. There were no intellectuals in my area who could put me in the direction of poetry. I was the only person in my family who read and painted and made sculptures. I grew up relatively isolated and my contact with books was with only the most traditional ones. I didn't realise then how good this was for me. It was only later, aged nineteen or twenty, I went "across the river" to the Rusafa side and mixed with the 60s generation. Crossing that bridge became symbolic for so much in my life. There, on the other side, each group had its own café. There was one café for Communists, another for Trotskyites, and yet another for Maoists and then there were still others for Ba'thists, Pan-Arabists and so forth. One café named after the singer, Um Khalthoum, and yet another was for blind people, many of whom played their instruments there. Those cafés were a very important part of our culture, but in some ways it was a dark scene. All the time I kept asking, "Where is *my* café? Where's the café that represents my sense of perplexity and wonderment and separateness?" Everyone belonged to a political party or artistic direction. The writers who enthused about modernity behaved very much like ideologues, even to the extent of creating their own enemies. I could find no space between them. Those people of the 1960s with their readymade ideas remind me of the Russians of the 1860s. Dostoevsky wrote *The Devils* about them and so did Turgenev in his *Fathers and Sons*. Of course we didn't have a Dostoevsky or Turgenev in our culture who could give voice to these matters. Our situation was similar to theirs in that we too had our devils, real ones who with their crazy ideas sought to recreate the world on their level, who forced the people to think along similar lines, making them believe their problems could be resolved quickly through revolution. This is why Iraq was completely destroyed, and in the precisely the same way the Russian radicals of the 1860s were to blame so too were the Iraqi intellectuals of the 1960s. They pushed the poor people. The poor like to dream whereas the rich, with all their experience of life, like to play with reality. The poor came to believe the rich so that they themselves destroyed even the ditches you see in that photograph, which brought water to every house.'

There comes in the poem a strange passage in which Fawzi and a friend are in a boat near the bridge when they witness some turbulence: 'Yards away, some buckled chunk of shrapnel/smashes into the water's face.' It took me a couple of readings to determine where, chronologically, the reader is supposed to be. The temporal haze is deliberate. Although the scene is set in the early 1960s, the object the boys see arrives from thirty years or so in the future.

On 17 January 1991, at the beginning of the operation known as Desert Storm, Major Joe Salata flew his sleek, bat-like F-117A Nighthawk, which the Saudis nicknamed *Shabah* or 'Ghost', through Baghdad's night skies. At the dropping of those first bombs Salata made the utterance that was heard on news broadcasts all over the world and which reappears, slightly recast, in Fawzi's poem: 'The city lit up like a Christmas tree.' Grossly inappropriate though the image may be, it was not the first time people have located

93

beauty in destruction. Salata, speaking further of this event, says, 'I can remember one target in Baghdad – it was a bridge. My objective was to drop the bridge into the water. It wasn't to kill everybody on the bridge, but I saw a car starting to drive across the bridge, and I actually aimed behind him, so he could pass over the bridge. If I had hit the left side of the bridge, he would've driven right into the explosion. Instead I hit the right side. You can pick and choose a little bit in the F-117… I think the guy made it safely across the bridge, but you can't really think about that when you're at war. You could drive yourself crazy, thinking of those kind [sic] of things. If you have a target to hit, you hit it.' Joe Salata, only two years Fawzi's senior, made a perfect strike or what in military jargon is called 'placing steel on target'. The column of the bridge, around which Fawzi used to swim, becomes, in the poem, the image of an uprooted tree.

> It's time to deepen
>   the gulf left by the roots
> A tree uprooted grows tall.
> Vacating its place of planting,
>   it grows, and then it vanishes
> Like smoke:
> On the water's face
>   nothing but the shiver of a breeze.
> My friend and I are in a boat.
> We lean over and lift the shiver
> Off the face of the water,
>   making a net of our hands.
> The fish quiver, leap and vanish.

The bombing of that bridge was something Fawzi watched on television, in Greenford, and now, at a curious point in our history, where communication is both remote and intimate, a quick search on the internet reveals the name of he who fired the missile.

*

On 14 July 1958, when Fawzi was thirteen, General 'Abd al-Karim Qasim marched into Baghdad and within hours effectively put an end to Iraq's Hashemite Dynasty. The coup, which was welcomed by the majority of people, was one of the most savage in recent Arab history. The young King Faisal and twenty members of his family, including women and children, were butchered. The evening before, when the world seemed at peace, a Pakistani magician had put on a show for the children, among the entertainments a couple of trained turtle-doves, one of which pulled the other in a small cart. They flapped their wings and picked up small objects when told to. Where did those doves go? There is an Arabic term *sahel*, which means to humiliate a person by dragging his corpse through the street. *Sahel* was the Iraqi Revolution's guillotine. It became symbolic of what happens when a people temporarily, and collectively, goes insane. The corpse of the Crown Prince, 'Abd al-Ilah – 'hound of the imperialists', according to slogans of the time – after being cleaved of its hands and feet, was then mutilated and dragged over the Aliya Bridge to the gate of the Ministry of Defence where it was hanged. After the souvenir hunters had their way with it, there remained only a piece of backbone. Prime Minister Nuri al-Said ('lackey of the West'), who once rode with T.E. Lawrence, attempted to make his escape dressed as a woman but was spotted when the bottoms of his pyjamas showed beneath the *aba* or black gown. There is debate as to whether he was shot or committed suicide.

'It is very hard to speak of this because I did not fully understand what was going on. I was very young. They took Nuri's corpse, burnt it, dismembered it, dragged the pieces all over the streets of Baghdad for three days, and after that they hung them from the bridge. The burning thigh I saw with my own eyes, close to my house. All of us ran after it and started shouting revolutionary slogans but I returned home quickly because of the smell of the burning flesh. You can't imagine from where such hatred comes.'

> We saw the world with its trousers down and laughed.
> We opened vents for the smell in our shackled bodies
> And the smell disappeared within us.
> That revolutionary summer had just such a smell.
> And my father said, 'Whoever goes sniffing out corpses
>   would want to be rid of their stench.'

'And because I actually saw this, it came naturally into my poem although there, of course, it takes on a different hue, one that suits the imagination of someone like me. Most of what we have seen since in Iraq is a variation of what happened in the course of that single day. This event produced a great crisis in my unconscious.'

'You spoke earlier of having crossed the bridge to the 60s, yet you remain critical of them.'

'What happened with my generation happened everywhere. This is why I criticise the 60s altogether, whether they were in America or Paris or Iraq. That generation didn't look to the earth but rather to the stars which seemed so bright at the time.'

'Surely, though, the 60s in Iraq must have been very different.'

'Completely, but it *tried* to copy the 60s in the West. I am speaking of the intellectuals, of course. They were dreamers full of hate, whose great ideas went ultimately against humanity.'

'You speak of modern Arabic poetry as not being able to embrace the truth and as having become a vehicle for hate.'

'The ideological mind has a clear way. It knows where it ends. The Marxist sees clearly the future, which is why he urges people to look there and to neglect the past and present altogether. That's why our countries prefer anthems that sing of the future. This mind in order to give meaning to the struggle must create an enemy especially if there isn't one already there. It got so every idea in our society was a political one. You *had* to be Communist or Ba'thist or, in later years, Islamicist. If poetry does not have the capacity to build a party with guns and knives, then at least it can manipulate the emotions to inspire hatred. One of our best poets, 'Abd al-Wahhab al-Bayyati, wrote a line, "We will make ashtrays out of their skulls." Another poet wrote, "I made from the skin of my enemies a tent to shield myself from the sun" and yet another warns that when he gets hungry he will eat the flesh of his enemy. These may be strong images, but really they are the opposite of strength. They have nothing to do with *real* poetry.'

'Clearly you are outside the mainstream of modern Arabic poetry. When did that separation begin?'

'I think it was there from the beginning. My first collection of poems, *At the Beginning of All Things*, published in 1968, when I was twenty-four, did not speak of anything ordinarily dealt with at the time. Those poems as a whole were a kind of song without words, and as such constitute a brief romantic period in my creative life. The separation was already there, not because of the intellectual atmosphere or the life I was leading but because of something in my own nature.'

'You had a great mentor at that time.'

'Yes, the Iraqi poet, Badr Shakir al-Sayyab. I had been looking for new things, especially those coming from Europe via Beirut. Adonis was an important poet for me, but his brightness and greatness belonged not to my inner experience but to Modernism. There is nothing private, nothing as unique as the human. That is what *I* want from a poem. What I realise now is that the "newness" I was after had another name: *timelessness*. I get the "new" only when I start digging into the past. When one is young it is a beautiful thing to think about the world and to interpret it in a different way, but with experience the poet looks behind the surface, conversing with what is hidden there. Likewise, he writes his poem for the hidden reader. I am not *modern*. When finally I realised this, I went back to al-Sayyab. When I was young I would sit with my friends, most of whom were not writers, by the Tigris singing his poems, and even now I sing them. A great poet is one who can make dialogue with me. A poet with whom I am unable to do this is not *my* poet. Al-Sayyab became a Communist but later the Communists hurt him deeply and so he became a Pan-Arabist but, really, he didn't believe in either. He believed rather in his own weakness, his isolation among poets who thought of themselves as prophets. He died in 1964, aged thirty-eight, destroyed by everything – the politics, the intellectuals, the women, none of whom loved him although now some of them write memoirs about their warm relationship with him. He was someone who could elevate history with mythology such that even his village, Jaykour, has become a mythical place. If you mention Jaykour in Syria, they will say "This is the village of al-Sayyab." But it is not the Jaykour of real life. If you mention the Buwayb River everyone will tell you this is the river that runs through al-Sayyab's poetry, but if you go to Basra you'll find it is only a tiny stream. This river became for him a mythical thing, a part of his underground world which he could belong to rather than to this world.'

'You say the intellectuals were largely responsible for the country's demise.'

'We did not have journalists as such at that time. They were mostly intellectuals – poets, writers, or critics. They were the only ones who stood between culture and the people, between ideas and the people. Such ideas as ordinary people had were all taken from the media – TV, radio and newspapers – or else from the political parties, all of which were run by intellectuals. When I describe the café scene as terrible, it is because there were no people there, only ideas. There were answers but never any questions in those places and yet each coterie had its own answer as to what the truth is. I will give you an illustration. I had a good friend, a typical Communist writer, a very nice man whose ideas were so clearly put they didn't allow for questions. This friend was born in the al-Shawaka area of Baghdad. Baghdad has many districts which are either Sunni or Shi'a. So here we have al-Shawaka which is Shi'a and al-Juafir which is Sunni and separating them is a narrow street, al-Shuhada, which has a lot of doctors and pharmacies. When life was relaxed there was no difficulty between those two sides. When the ideological crisis came, al-Shawaka became Communist and al-Juafir became Pan-Arabist. The first preferred tomatoes because they are red, Communism's colour, and the second preferred cucumbers because they are green, the colour of the Pan-Arabist movement. I said to my friend, "Try to use your imagination. Suppose you were born fifteen metres away from here, just across the road, what do you think you would have become? You would have been a pan-Arabist, not a Communist! You are seventy now and you have clung to this illusion simply because, satisfied with readymade answers, you want to be free of having to ask questions. Yet so many people were killed for this illusion."'

'This brings us to the subject of your first escape from Iraq.'

'When the Ba'thists came to power in 1968, I went to Beirut. At that time I left my job as a teacher of Arabic, which I had greatly enjoyed. A lot of boys became good readers simply because I was with them for those nine months. The secret police came to my school, asking questions about me. At that time the Ba'thists began to focus on teachers, and because I was neither Communist nor Ba'thist I was more suspect. If I were taken into custody, there would have been no party behind me. I was accused of stepping outside my lessons and of talking to my students about philosophy and literature. This was my style of teaching. I talked about Arabic writers and because my students lived far from the centre of Baghdad, I brought them books. A number of students whose families were Ba'thist informed on me. They said I spoke about the devil or the angel and that I had caused them to stray from their studies or that I had advised them to read certain writers. They accused me of being a liberal – *librale* – which was a very dangerous accusation because to be liberal meant that one belonged not to any single ideology, Ba'thism or Communism, but to the West. Luckily for me, a relative of mine was then head of the Department of Education and had all the records on me. He warned me to take care, saying information was being gathered on me. So I went to Beirut. My family knew nothing about it. I was twenty-four at the time. I had already published my first book in Baghdad and so I was known in Beirut. Also I was published there in *Sh'ir* and *al-Adab* magazines. At first Beirut was a paradise. It was like Paris. I read Sartre, Camus and Eliot although I didn't really know how to be modern. I went deeply into things that were never really part of my inner life. It was like watching a lovely American film in darkness and then stepping out into the light and seeing life as it really was. I stayed in Beirut for two and a half years. The poet Yusuf al-Khal was there. Adonis helped me. But a lot of things in Beirut began to destroy me. I started to drink. Alcohol was cheap. Then, in 1971–2, in Iraq there was a coalition between the Ba'thists and Communists. There was a sense of relief and that maybe now things would get better. So I returned there.'

The story of that return provides what in the poem feels like a sweet hell of dissolution of endless booze, of evenings spent in debate at the Gardenia Tavern, now long gone, which in Fawzi's writings has become a kind of spiritual home, and of sleeping rough on park benches.

> The waiter sees the mud on my galoshes
> And sweat, from a wank, on my brow.
> A reek, as from the underwings of bats,
>   wafts out, freed from my armpits.
> The waiter tries to head me off.
> Ah, but the summer urges me
> To trample fields not trampled on before
> Or take the shape of a beast from another time.

The irony is that for Fawzi and others of his generation it was a kind of blighted paradise, a hallucinogenic lull before all hell broke loose.

'Yes, but it wasn't such a hell really. Compared to what would follow, it was rather beautiful at that time. We had a safe, if brief, existence. After we left the taverns the best thing was to sleep outside beside the river. This was normal. That was a good period in our history. After the British companies left, the money from the oil was all ours. The Ba'thists showed another face, although at that time I knew Saddam, this man who when he was sixteen killed his own cousin, to be a filthy man. The Communists had to defend him, saying this was *our* man. Only a couple of years later, Saddam's black cars, eight of them, without licence plates, with black curtains in the windows, became a symbol of terror. They drove everywhere at high speed, and from any one of those cars men would leap out and grab somebody, taking him God knows where. If anyone went near one of those cars, he would be arrested. People had no idea if Saddam was in any of them or not. Saddam's name became more important and terrifying than the President's. I knew this man would be the realisation of all my darkest fears.'

'You must have witnessed many tragedies, writers who thought they could embrace one ideology or another and were subsequently destroyed by those choices.'

'They paid no attention to the idea of truth, even if there wasn't any truth to be found, or to the idea of asking questions even if there were no answers. I broke with a couple of friends when they joined the Ba'thists. On the other hand I had many Ba'thist friends, a couple of whom protected me several times, but they were mostly people who were in it from the beginning and not like those who later became Ba'thist just so they could have money and power. These people I avoided. The Revolution destroyed people. People were murdered or else killed themselves.

> My generation's had to put up
> With its fair share of knocks.
> One hid his head inside a shell
> And lived below the surface for a while;
>
> Another died within his coat as he tore at his insides
> In a country where brigades of fans
> Just blow away the dunes

'There is nothing I can say about the people I knew that wouldn't apply to the many thousands of others who died. Actually, most of my friends died of other causes, drink, for example. I dedicated my *Collected Poems* to twelve people, some of whom were killed, others who simply died young, but I say all of them were *killed*. They were victims.'

One poet Fawzi remembers in particular is 'Abd al-Amir al-Husairi whom he describes as 'the hero of his own dream'. This *poète maudit* has come to represent for Fawzi and for others of his generation the dying gasp of a Romanticism that may owe more to the bottle than to verse. Al-Husairi came from Najaf which is one of the centres of religious learning, home to the Imam 'Ali Mosque, whose resplendent dome is made of 7,777 golden tiles, and which for Shi'a is the third holiest shrine in existence. For a young poet deeply rooted in classical Arabic literature, the move, in 1959, from such a pious atmosphere to Baghdad, now capital of revolution, was a traumatic one. In a new world that demanded of every intellectual that he be aglow with ideological passion, al-Husairi, oblivious to the political circus, saw only that life was increasingly getting worse for most people.

'A very talented poet, he was surrounded by some of the best writers of the time. A Romantic, which is how I see myself; that is, belonging to a struggle that involves the duality between freedom and necessity, individuality and responsibility, al-Husairi was, symbolically speaking, the last of his kind. We all drank, of course. Alcohol was an important dimension of any poet at that time. If al-Husairi drank more heavily than us, it was probably because he didn't belong to anything and so, in his alienation, drank all the more. A man of dreams, he was in despair, and finally the drink swallowed him. He lived in a cheap hotel in al-Maydan and every morning he would begin his journey from there, across Baghdad, to Abu Nuwas Street where our Gardenia Tavern was. You need at least an hour and a half, walking in a straight line, to get from where he was to where we were. It took much longer, of course, because he stopped at every bar on the way. Everybody in those bars knew and accepted him. "Here comes al-Husairi!" they'd say and so he would sit with them, drinking one or two glasses of *arak* before moving on, and so, stopping at each place, he would finally come to us at the Gardenia. He would settle there for a while, very proud inside his dream, and spoke like a god, and this we accepted although we wouldn't have done so from anyone else. Then he would continue the rest of his journey by the end of which he would have consumed roughly two litres of *arak*. We all knew that one day soon we would hear of his death. When it came, in 1973, he was still a young man. The great thing about this character was that everybody, even the ordinary people on the street, knew him. This popularity was of a kind that has completely vanished from Baghdadi existence. Al-Husairi was the last glimpse of a great period now gone forever. He was the scion of a great village called Iraq. I did a drawing of him naked.

'With regard to this recurring image of nakedness in my work, I did a large painting once, of an imaginary festival in Baghdad, which depicts a brass band playing, people dancing, people preparing food as if for a special occasion, and in it everybody is naked. Why naked? The naked ones are the dead coming back to life and what you have in the painting is a whole city putting on this great festival in order to receive them. When I drew al-Husairi naked, I believe I did so unconsciously. This is how the image came to me: *he was naked because he was dead*. When I make drawings of al-Sayyab, I also do him naked. So nakedness for me is an image of something coming from another world, from death itself. I even did a painting of myself naked in a room, with a bottle of wine.'

'And then, of course, there were those who went the other way.'

'You need to be very sensitive and talented in order to feel deeply about this tragedy. Most people weren't. Others simply became bad people. I do not wish to mention them by name. Still others tried to get on as best as possible. I will give you another example. One of my friends is a good short story writer who writes about the inner struggles of people, or about the struggles between them and their fate, or about their condition, which is that of always looking for the light. One of his stories is about a man seeking death because for him the height of desire is to vanish. We had all these voices, saying life's problems could be resolved through ideas and ideologies, and then along comes this writer who speaks about things which are so deep. This is what writing should do, teach us how to live. Anyway, it was impossible for such a man to involve himself with politics. At that time Saddam started to support writers, often giving them expensive gifts or money. Saddam sent my friend a Mercedes-Benz. A car in Baghdad is very expensive to run and the Mercedes-Benz was worth more than his house. This was a gift from Saddam, so what could he do? He couldn't refuse this gift coming from someone so terrible. Also he couldn't drive. He couldn't give the car to anyone else to drive nor could he sell it because if the secret police found out he'd be in trouble. So he moved the car inside his house and from then on he spent much of his time on it, cleaning it every two or three days because it was not good to leave the engine. He did this for a couple of years and, after a while, when the tyres started to sag from disuse, he propped the car up on stones. All this was just so he could avoid problems. Chekhov could have written a story about this nightmare. It is such a dark and beautiful theme, what the Russians call "a smile between tears", and all this poor man could do was grimace.'

*

Fawzi, it has to be said, is a good cook. It must have taken him ages to stuff the tomatoes, peppers and courgettes with herb-infused meat and rice, a Baghdadi specialty. Our move to the dinner table, in a room flooded with light, where a wasp flew in circles, also provided a natural turning point in our conservation, which now focused on his decision to leave Baghdad forever.

'I did so because I wanted to survive. I desired another language, true, but this was not the main thing that drove me out. It was in order to survive. When I returned from Beirut I wrote for a weekly magazine. I received a fixed wage, although I was not formally employed, either as a worker or a journalist. I preferred this. If I wanted to leave the country, however, I had to get written permission from my head of department, which I couldn't do because I wasn't working officially. So I persuaded a Ba'thist friend to ask the director who, by the way, was a well-known poet, to give me this paper granting me leave to travel for two weeks. My friend tried several times and each time was refused, the director's excuse being that once I was on the outside I'd write a poem against the regime.

He said this even though he knew I wasn't a political writer! One day, without realising it, he signed the paper. It was the end of the day, and he wanted to go home, and so, without looking at them, he hurriedly signed all the papers in front of him. The following morning a nice old man who brought us tea said, "Fawzi, this is for you." I told my friend, and he said, "Don't tell anyone!" I got my passport in a couple of days.

My friend, take off your shoes.
Take off your shoes and go barefoot,
For this is the last time we tread
The ground of our country.
Tomorrow the footwear of exile will fit us both.

'First I went to Paris which is "the city of light", where everything's on the outside. Paris, the Latin Quarter in particular, is traditionally the first choice of Arab intellectuals. I stayed there for a month. I can't criticise Paris which, after all, is the heart of Europe. I had come from Baghdad, which was very poor and simple, to the great city of Sartre, Camus, Rimbaud and Mallarmé. But I didn't really like it there. The French are so very fashionable, changing all the time, and with the Arabs it's the same. Every couple of years or so, we have a new school of thinking. I hate all that. *My* time does not move. In Arabic we call it *dhar* or, in English, "eternal time". When I came to Dover the policeman asked me, "Why are you visiting Britain?" I didn't have the English words with which to answer him. "Holiday?" he asked. Still I couldn't understand, so I started looking for a small dictionary I'd brought with me. I couldn't find it. "OK, OK," he said, "You're on holiday," and let me pass. It was like a dream. When I arrived at Victoria Station, I knew immediately this was my city. I felt something here embrace me. I had left a country where I spent five years in darkness, which was not safe, where anything could happen to you. I was frightened, of course. Again I go back to those two trees. Paris is the mulberry tree, full of light, all my friends sitting and chatting in the cafés, while London is the oleander where everything is wet and dark or else hidden behind walls. When I begin to compare them, I can see why I love London more. It's because it brings me to myself, to what is deep inside me, and to what I need. Here was a country which had Romanticism for 200 years and also there were the same red double-decker buses that we had in Baghdad. I worked as a proofreader for an Arabic newspaper. I didn't work as a journalist, which was a good thing because I didn't have to mix my poetic with journalistic language. I started writing articles on music. I got a bicycle. I had one in Baghdad. It was not often you saw a poet on a bicycle there. They called me "Abu Bicycle". With time, I came to love London in a real way and also, of course, the English language. London is a very generous city. If I belong to any city, it is this one. I appreciate its humanistic side even though, in 1981, I was attacked and badly beaten by skinheads in Earls Court. I was on the way home from seeing *Rigoletto*, carrying my bright red programme. There are bad people everywhere. This city gave me, for the first time in my life, a place to live. In Baghdad I lived in cheap hotels, seedy rooms in poor areas. And then, in the first year I was here, I had a serious heart attack. My friends said, "You fled Iraq only for this to happen?" I lost all hope. I felt this was the end of life. Strangely, though, this awful experience greatly benefited me. Maybe it gave me more than life itself gave me. Death had come so simply. The word became real, maybe deeper than reality itself. All of us speak about death, but really it's only words. What is the difference between words and experience? You may have a lot of things but not the fruit that comes from them. A great man may know death without experiencing it – he does not need to be on a deathbed to understand that without death life is nothing and that it can push the poet or thinker onto a road of knowledge and wisdom that previously had seemed inaccessible.'

'You say you have not been able to swim in English time.'

'Sometimes I feel I am not really living here and that for these past thirty years I have been inside a great library. I go to the shelves, remove a book, and then replace it. I may enjoy this, but it is not really life. I think that in order to feel he is alive a writer needs to know that somebody somewhere is talking to him. A reader who likes what I write *speaks* with me. Maybe this is what I have lost or what I miss most living here. I am not English. I do not *live* among English people. I do not have English friends. I met some English poets, but with them it was mainly sitting and talking arbitrarily about things on the outside, nothing ever really in depth, and then nobody contacts you afterwards. Still I don't feel I'm so terribly isolated because my close friends are books and music. I need at least double this life to obtain half of what I want. This isolation is not life, however, and maybe to say I am living in a great library sounds a shade dramatic. Sometimes, though, I feel I am waiting, like Godot, at a train stop. A train comes every minute, full of people, and there is no space for me. So it is very hard to speak about this and to which time I belong when I don't belong to any. Maybe this is the tragic side of my life or, because I feel it so deeply, it might even be the most enjoyable side. The richest part of my intellectual life has been spent here. Modern English poetry is still hard for me, and much of what I see is, I think, very provincial. You need to be a Londoner to understand a London poet. I am involved with a metaphysical dimension, which is why I prefer poets like Czesław Miłosz who are similarly engaged. Only there, in that dimension, do I find someone to speak to.'

'When you first came here, did it take a while to find your poetic voice again?'

'I think I stayed silent for just one or two years, but then I busied myself with a lot of other things. I studied language, and I tried to read English books. When you first came here from Canada it was, in a sense, like going from one village to another, both of which had similar cultures, the same poets and the same philosophers, but coming from a place like Baghdad meant I had to cross a much deeper divide. And now my friends are dead or else they have become old and the places I knew are gone, the Gardenia Tavern, for example.'

The Gardenia belongs to Fawzi's massive store of images. When he returned to Baghdad for the first time, in 2004, he found it closed and it has become yet another place which he can revisit only in painting and verse. It is the subject of one of his most powerful canvases. The empty space at the lower right-hand corner is where al-Husairi should be.

'When I say my time is gone, I speak as a poet. It is not difficult for me to go to Damascus and to re-enter Arabic time, which means just happily sitting there and watching, and thinking about nothing at all, and going towards nowhere in particular. I need this some-times, but I couldn't live there. Anyway, as you said to me earlier, Arabic time is disappearing – it is being replaced by world time.'

'Away from your audience, what enables you, or pushes you, to write? Who are you writing for?'

'Sometimes I feel I write for nobody at all but at least in some corner of this world, and I have experienced this several times, there are people who read my poems and like them and feel they have a dialogue with them.'

'So maybe being here has helped you.'

'It has helped me a lot! If we both understand what we mean by the word "exile", I am not an exile in the way many people like to think. I'd sooner say I was already an exile in Iraq when I began to write. I felt language to be an obstacle, and not a thing I needed, and that it was impossible to push language all the way to its roots. Often I tell people if I could be anything else it would be a composer and this is because music is abstract and as such it is where my passion and my struggles lie. Words alone just won't do it for me. When dealing with language, a poet has certain problems because the words he uses are the words everybody else uses. We know language is the only tool of communication between people. So I come to words, wishing to use them in a completely different way, but will the language go easily with me? Will she accept me as a visitor and allow me to use her differently from, say, how a scientist does? The important point here is that rather than settle for the language we all use, I dream of going back to its very roots, to the very origins of language. When a human begins to give expression to something he starts with movement – words come later. At the beginning there was no gap between the word and the thing it describes. With time, that gap became bigger and bigger and the words became symbols for many other things as well. So when a poet deals with language, he dreams about returning to its source, when the word *was the thing*, but already he is an exile because there is a gap between the thing said and what he desires. He struggles to close this gap, but it is impossible. This is the first dimension of exile. If we go to another dimension, another level of exile, here you are, someone who thinks and feels and sees differently from the people around you. This is the problem between the individual as poet and his society. It's not easy really. When I was quite young I dropped everything and went to Beirut. Most of my dreams at that time contained my mother and father because I hadn't finished with them, I still needed them, but I needed to leave too. So this, in addition to the other two I have just described, was another form of exile. When I returned to Baghdad, I knew something was forcing me. It wasn't really a matter of choice. It was partly the illusion that everything there was about to improve, the political coalition being a new step towards paradise, but I knew this to be foolish. Also, I needed to return because I was tired of Beirut and of being without work or money. All the while I knew it would be going back to hell and so, for another six or seven years, I struggled inside this hell. The other day I wrote a poem in which time becomes a boat on the Tigris and it goes with the current to the sea and there vanishes completely. So I came to London. I watch the Thames here, full of boats and with no space for any smaller ones between them. It is not my time at all. That's why I say it is not so bad to live without time. And this is what I mean about exile inside language, that there is some great source which is forever lost. We are exiled from the origins of language. So it's not really true when I say I have written a new poem. There is no *new* poem. One just repeats things, adding a little bit here and there to the great store of poetry that has been available since *Gilgamesh*. If the "new" happens, it does so only on the surface or with technical matters. For thirty years now, I have had this familiarity with English or Western poetry – I do not differentiate between England and the rest of Europe because for me the West is one huge country. If I have familiarised myself with Western art and poetry and philosophy and music, and I'm still pursuing things as yet unknown to me, I have failed to do the same with people themselves. I think this is not only a very deep exile but also a tragedy. And – this is the terrible thing – I enjoy it! If I could choose, if I could be familiar with the people who love their culture, it would be great thing, but it seems impossible now, especially at my age. This is hard for me and yet this gives me depth and courage.

I do not feel I am dealing with ordinary things but with the exceptional. So it is not necessarily a negative exile. When I think about exile, it is not in the ordinary sense of the word. It is one of many dimensions. I remember once looking at a map of the universe, with its millions of galaxies, surrounded by this great darkness from which it is impossible to derive any answers, and I felt there was no space for our galaxy with its sun and earth and of course there was no space for me. This gave me a deep sense of universal exile. Suddenly I felt this great loneliness and a sense of no longer being safe. It was as if I were a child seeing his house for the first time without his father and mother. This sense of not belonging anywhere is what provided me with the first glimpse of a metaphysical dimension.'

'And being surrounded by the English language, has that in some way helped purify your Arabic?'

'Yes, the English language has greatly benefited me, not just with the logical structure of its sentences but also, most importantly, with its sense of justice. In Arabic, there are many words which I'd call "unjust". For example, often when we speak about something or someone we'll automatically add '*ala al-itlaq*, which means "absolutely". We use this word all the time and yet it doesn't allow space for either the speaker or the listener to understand his limitations. What is said in Arabic is so abstract, so boundless, whereas in English you don't employ more words than you require. This has affected my poetry, which is why when I return to my old poems I see in them a lot of meaningless space. They're full of words without meaning. I already gave you a couple of examples of strong images, which to my mind merely denote hate. This is something we have in our language. The poet says what he does not really mean, which has nothing to do with his experience, and which he himself does not believe. It is not necessary for him to believe in what he says but rather to give a strong image. That is why our great classical poet al-Mutanabbi is full of these lies. They may be powerful images, but I read them as expressions of strong hate. This is what I mean by justice. As a consequence of being here, I have become very close to the idea of the simple sentence, one in which there is no exaggerated feeling or idea or belief. It is better to leave things just as they are. Once you add these other things you misjudge, you become *unjust*. The Arabic poetry of the last forty years has become so empty, such that with many books you can't even get past their titles. You then go inside them and there is no solid basis of knowledge, no dialogue with surrounding experience, nothing there is *settled*, and yet the language stays afloat like a balloon, growing inside itself. There is no weight of human experience. This covers almost 70 per cent of Arabic writing in that it is artificial and empty. You have these modernists imitating New York, and even now, in these terrible times, they are speaking in the same tone. This is the height of carelessness. It is not necessary for Baghdad to become Paris in order to write good poetry there. This is the story of my struggle with Arab intellectuals, which is why most of my books do not go down well with them.'

We barely quarried the mountain of food Fawzi made. There was enough to see him through for a week or so. We moved back into the relative darkness of his living room where I suggested we end where we began, with the painting of him swimming in the Tigris, which depicts him as an older man rather than the child he was when he last swam there.

'Painting for me is a relaxation from writing poems. Writing makes me tense, whereas painting is like going for a walk in wide open spaces. It is a working of the soul and body together. Some friends of mine who are painters say this is not painting in the way they understand it because usually one starts from colours, shapes and lines. They say I know how it will end in advance. This is not strictly true, but always the *image* is the first thing to come to me. I remember that the sense I had while painting this was of a man dreaming he is still swimming in the Tigris. As I said before, I do not live as others do, inside a current of ordinary time. You can see in the upper corner of the painting a wooden boat, called *belem* in the local dialect, which at that time was a principal means of river transport. Those boats are no longer in existence. Saddam forbade their use. The secret police destroyed my brother's boat and then beat him. The water in this painting has a double nature. It reflects a richness of life which at the same time is horrible. It is like the Will of Schopenhauer, a blind force that gives life and death at the same time. When you read Sumerian literature, the water there has another life. In the marshes in the south of Iraq, where the Tigris and the Euphrates meet, you get this still water, the stillness making it seem all that much darker. The ancient Sumerians believed it was at that place one crossed over to another world. It was where, each year, the god Thammuz began his great voyage to the underworld. Al-Sayyab felt instinctively that this water was a current of hidden time. It is pretty much the same with the water in my poetry. I call these paintings "the poet's mirror". Sometimes what he sees is devilish in nature, a madman with a dark figure behind him or a naked man sitting in a strange, empty room with his bottle of wine. I think you can deal with these paintings in the same way you deal with my poems.'

'Would you ever go back to Iraq to live?'

'I don't think so. Even if everything settles down in Iraq, and I go back there to live, I'd swim in a time that has nothing to do with me any more. At the same time, this encourages me. It gives my poetry a new dimension. The idea that my time is dead is not really such a bad one. I have not swum in English time either. A friend of mine, a good writer, tells me this is wrong, that I must belong to what I have now. "You should write in English," he tells me. Maybe he is right, but even if that were possible I don't think I could give in English what I can still give in Arabic. The fact that I can give at all is because I am in a void. This is no bad thing. Most people need time. A poet doesn't need time.'

Always the gentleman, and also because a dicky heart requires he take exercise, Fawzi put on his cream summer blazer which, maybe because of his dark complexion, makes him look so handsome, and accompanied me to Greenford Station where, uniquely for London, although commonplace for those who live there, one goes up to the train platform on a wooden escalator which has been granted, to the joy of rail enthusiasts everywhere, a stay of execution. This, too, was a journey outside time.

Marius Kociejowski

Notes on the Poems

P. 13

al-Khidr   A mythical personage alluded to in the Quran. He walked on water. In his memory, Iraqis light candles and place them on plates made of rushes which they float down the Tigris.

The flood   In spring, the Tigris is in spate.

Gilgamesh   Gilgamesh is a mythical king, the hero of the great national epic of Iraq.

P. 14

But there are the cats   For a considerable section of the first and of the last part of *Plague Lands* the poet utilises an ancient form of cadence – called the *rajaz* – which evokes the sound of horses' hooves: *Fa'aloun, Fa'aloun, Fa'aloun* etc. I have attempted to suggest this rhythm here.

P. 15

I read The Book of Beasts *by al-Jahiz*   I might have put this thus:

> I read the *Kitab al-Hayawan* by al-Jahiz
> And in the *Wafayat al-A'yan*
> And in *al-Mustatraf* I read deeply,
> The *Thamarat al-Awraq* by my side...

The poet cites the names of these well-known works of ancient Arabic literature not so much for their significance as for the music of their titles. But then we would lose the humour of the imaginary titles he then claims for himself.

The margin   Arabic manuscripts often contain two texts: a principal text, and one in the margin, distinct from the first.

P. 16

a stiff arak   The word for the alcholic spirit also means 'sweat' in Arabic.

The roasting of a thigh   The prime minister of Iraq was lynched and burnt during the revolution of 14 July, 1958. One of his legs was dragged along by the demonstrators – who passed close to the house of the poet.

P. 17

Summer shows Baghdad in its true colours   Iraqi *coups d'état* always occur in the summer.

The ninth-century Ibn al-Rumi, as distinct from Rumi the Sufi poet, was a Rabelaisian figure and a major satirist. Abu Nuwas was a ninth-century poet who admired male ephebes and courtesans' behinds. Abu al-Tayyib al-Mutanabbi (referred to simply as al-Tayyib in the poem) is a major poet of the tenth century at the court in Aleppo of Saif al-Dawla. Many of the other poets mentioned, including al-Baghdadi, Ibn Nabata, al-Sallami, Ibn Sokara and Ibn al-Hajjaj are 'marginal' poets of the tenth and eleventh centuries. Renowned, or castigated, for their black humour, they led dissipated lives, for the most part, while offering unhesitant criticism of society and power.

Saqt al-Zand   'Flint-sparks', by al-Ma'arri, a great poet and a philosopher.

Shorja   The *souk* of Baghdad.

P. 18

Neither our crown prince nor caliph   A classical form of versification is used here, admitting of two readings – following either the margin or the indentation – or this is how I have attempted to render it in English.

P. 20

It sets forth blithe as a girl   Quoted from a pre-Islamic poem by Omar Ibn Ma'ado Karb.

P. 21

And the hangings stretched across the Eastern Gate   While this passage alludes to Turkish atrocities of previous centuries, it is worth noting that of the seven gates of ancient Baghdad, this gate has a great circular gathering space where demonstrations often take place. Since 1968, the corpses of more than thirty people have been hung there, often on the pretext of espionage.

P. 22

Variations on a theme dear to Rilke and Miłosz: the callousness of nature as opposed to the hypersensitivity of the soul.

Pp. 24 and 25
Gilgamesh/Enkidu For Gilgamesh, see note to p. 13. Enkidu is the companion of Gilgamesh, whose brute nature is to some extent tamed by society.

P. 39
I get in touch with its djinni Or genie – as in Aladdin's lamp. This passage is inspired by Faust and one of the *Three Tales* in the film by Antonioni. It concerns the temptation of a pact with the devil. Fawzi Karim is an authority on Western classical music.

P. 45
The Jumhouriyya Bridge 'The Bridge of the Republic', one of the most beautiful bridges over the Tigris. The poet would take this bridge to cross over to the bars of Abu Nuwas Street. It was hit in 1991, during the First Gulf War. From the bridge's apex, one can see Bab al-Sharqi, the open space by the Eastern Gate, which was the scene of the hangings alluded to in Part 1.

P. 46
al-Abbasiyya no longer exists al-Abbasiyya was the old quarter of Baghdad, on the right bank of the Tigris. Situated between the old parliament building and the presidential palace, it was one of the first districts to be demolished by the powers that were. The waters of the Tigris were forbidden since the palace and the homes of those in power gave onto the water.

P. 51
I drift from Bab al-Mu'adhem toward al-Maydan Square Bab al-Mu'adhem is one of the western gates of Baghdad, where universities are to be found as well as the Ministry of Defence. Al-Maydan Square was once the location for brothels and cabarets. It now has a few cafés and a bus station.

P. 52
The Ba'thists got him Zaïm – 'Leader' – was the title of President Kassim, chief of the liberating officers who led the revolution of 1958. He was killed in 1963 in a coup instigated by the Ba'thist party. Saddam Hussein participated in his murder. The Zaïm was popular and close to the people and held in affection by the poor.

There was a rumour that he was still alive. To cut this short, the Ba'thist generals exhibited his bullet-riddled corpse on television.

P. 54
Opera house   Covent Garden.

P. 68
Abu Hayyan   Abu Hayyan al-Tawhidi (c. 930–1023) was an Arabic litterateur and philosopher, probably of Persian origin.

P. 71
punka   A fan, mainly associated with India, made of a palm frond or strip of cloth hung from the ceiling and operated by a servant. In Iraq, the word is commonly used for an electric fan.

A Note on my Version

I speak no Arabic and have never translated from a language I speak. I translate in order to get in touch with a poem. If I can read it in the original there is no need to go through this process. In 1970, I did version of the pre-Islamic poet Imru'al-Qays, and, in an *apology* fc my presumption in making use of an English crib I discovered, stated that my correct version was the best poetry I could get out o' any passage. I have been guided by the same principle in this attem to render into English the poetry of Fawzi Karim, working mainl from a literal translation made into English by Abbas Kadhim. I am also grateful to Saadi Simawe and Melissa Brown for their translations of several of the shorter poems.

Anthony Howell